The DEVIL

What the Scriptures
teach about him

John Wesley White

TYNDALE
HOUSE PUBLISHERS, INC.
Wheaton, Illinois

COVERDALE
HOUSE PUBLISHERS, LTD.
Eastbourne, England

Library of Congress Catalog Card Number 76-58130. ISBN 0-8423-0663-3, paper. Copyright © by Tyndale House Publishers, Inc., Wheaton, Illinois. All rights reserved. First printing, March 1977. Printed in the United States of America.

CONTENTS

Foreword

Man's fiercest foe, from the Garden of Eden right to the end of time, is not cancer, communism, disease, or death. It is the devil! He is the author of all evil. He is behind all our individual woes and international wars. He instigates all our crime and violence. He is the motivator of man's immorality—drunkenness, burglaries, adulteries, embezzlements, rapes, murders, assassinations, and hijackings. He writes the script for human sorrows, sickness, and death itself.

When I pray or preach the gospel of Jesus Christ publicly or privately, in the stadium or on international television, I am always aware of two supernatural powers at work: the power of the Holy Spirit who propels the Word of God, and the power of Satan who opposes it. Jesus told us that the devil's work in the world includes a constant effort to devour the disseminated

FOREWORD

Word lest the hearers should believe and be saved.

A generation ago, when I began as an evangelist, people generally and intellectuals in particular thought of the devil as an anachronistic symbol, a handy expression of profanity, or as a superstition— believed in chiefly by obscurantists and religious eccentrics. Today the devil is getting maximal exposure, precisely as the Bible predicted would happen prior to Christ's return. In theaters around the world some years ago *The Exorcist* broke all box office records, grossing 150 million dollars. It was followed by *Exorcism's Daughter, The Demons, Satan is Coming, The Legions of Lucifer,* and *The Devil's Wedding Night.*

In *The Devil* John Wesley White explores what the Bible has to say about Satan: where he came from, why he is in the world today, how he works, how he can be overcome, and where he is going. He does so with many quotations from the easy-to-read and easily understood *Living Bible* which has been such a blessing to so many millions of English-speaking people.

John Wesley White is a Canadian, holding his Doctor of Philosophy degree from Oxford University in England. I asked him in 1961 to become one of my associate evangelists. In that capacity he has traveled to a hundred countries, holding areawide crusades in which he has preached to an aggregate of two and a half million people, with some seventy-five thousand coming forward to make decisions for Christ. He has authored eight books and served for ten years as Chancellor (and hockey coach) of Richmond College in Toronto, where he lives with his wife, Kathleen, and four sons. With George Beverly Shea and Lowell Jackson, he has for several years been the speaker on our weekly Canadian television program, "Agape."

It is my prayer that through your reading of *The Devil*, you may better know, love, and serve the living Christ.

Billy Graham
June 1976

CHAPTER ONE

The Devil in Big Red Headlines

The devil! We all wish he'd go away! But he's around today a lot more than he was yesterday. And he's going to be more visible and vocal tomorrow than he is today, like a vast, vicious virus that won't stop. His iniquitous vices and ubiquitous devices are on every hand. To be ignorant of his attack tactics is to lay ourselves open to chronic peril.

One of the frequently interviewed people on television talk shows during the mid-seventies has been Arthur Lyons. His theme is the same as the title of his book, *The Second Coming: Satanism in America.* He makes the point that from a scientific or secular point of view, one of the least expected sensations of the seventies would have been a revival of a widespread belief in Satan, the current turning to devil worship and every conceivable form of witchcraft, black and white magic, spiritism, sorcery, and astrology. Who in the mainstream of Western thought a generation ago would have predicted that ahead lay a reaccreditation of the supernatural? Intellectuals were predicting that within a few years hardly anyone would believe in the existence of a personal devil.

Then as we entered the seventies, the polls began registering a strange new phenomenon: people right across the spectrum were saying openly that Satan was a reality. Two or three years later, Walter Cronkite was telling us on his "CBS Evening News" that belief in a personal devil had increased 11 percent in a decade. People began expressing belief in a literal Lucifer in pop song lyrics, in art, in the theatre, in the social sciences, in a whole new proliferation of religious cults; yes, and throughout academe.

But one thing is evident. *The Second Coming: Satanism in America* should not be a surprise to those who take the Bible seriously. "The Holy Spirit tells us clearly that in the last times," wrote St. Paul to Timothy, people would "turn away from Christ and become eager followers of teachers with devil-inspired ideas" (1 Timothy 4:1).

The Bible refers to that period surrounding the return of Christ as "the latter times," "the time of the end," and "the last days." Almost 2,000 verses of Scripture describe events and prevailing conditions which would characterize society at that "time of the end." From a multitude of fragments it is possible to piece together a picture of man and his world prior to the second coming of Jesus Christ, something obviously beyond the scope of this book.

One of the unmistakable signs of Christ's second coming is the outbreak of Satanism which confronts us today. It is a trend which inevitably will become more and more pronounced as the return of Christ draws nearer. Before and during the period of the "great tribulation" to which Jesus alluded (Matthew 24:21, KJV), the accelerating wind of Satan's activity will become a hurricane of diabolical harassment. "This great Dragon—the ancient serpent called the devil, or Satan" will become enraged as he sees his own ultimate downfall approaching. Having lost a "war in heaven," he is "thrown down onto the earth with all his army.... Woe to you people of the world, for the devil has come down to you in great anger, knowing that he has little time" (Revelation 12:7-12). Knowing that his time is short, he will mobilize and deploy all the forces at his evil command.

The prospect of such a thing is terrifying—but it is in sight now! Rampaging crime, revolution, war, hatred—even the talk of peace when there is no peace—are signs! Paul warned the Thessalonians, "What about the coming again of our Lord Jesus Christ?... That day will not come until two things happen: first, there will be a time of great rebellion against God, and then the man of rebellion will come—the son of hell... This man of sin will come as Satan's tool, full of satanic power" (2 Thessalonians 2:1, 3, 9).

Sometimes we think Satan's power is most evident in the squalid and superstitious flotsam of the inner cities and in pagan tribal societies. We also see it among dropouts who have become wandering drug addicts, perhaps occupying a cave somewhere out in the hills. But an incredible number of reports of satanic activity are coming from university professors and vocational religionists. Dr. Andrew Greeley of the University of Chicago points to the constant "attempts of the satanists to blend their doctrine with Enlightenment rationalism and evolutionary and scientific secularity." The current rage for parapsychology has brought accredited courses on satanism into universities where studies of the teachings of Jesus Christ are barred on the basis of separation of church and state. It is one of the ironies of our time.

Paul predicted that we would find malcontents in this "time when people won't listen to the truth, but will go around looking for teachers who will tell them just what they want to hear. They won't listen to what the Bible says but will blithely follow their own misguided ideas" (2 Timothy 4:3, 4). That precisely describes what is happening in many universities today: an eager curiosity about Satan, an interest most dangerous because it is packaged in sophisticated intellectualism.

The rebellion of the youth and students on nearly every continent the last few years seems to be prophesied by the Apostles Peter and Jude. Peter indicated that "false teachers" will be "turning against even their Master who bought them" (2 Peter 2:1).

The popularity of certain "entertainment" seems to prove this. An Ann Landers column in the Los Angeles *Herald Examiner* of June 23, 1972, pointed with disgust to a "weirdo-freak superstar who comes out loaded with jewelry, dressed like a dame and does this creepy number where he chops off a doll's head and make-believe blood oozes all over the stage. The psycho hangs himself at the close of the act." Miss Landers condemned this emphatically, but conceded, "The mail ran ten to one against us." The mobs of the 1970s would undoubtedly repeat the first century cry, "Away with him! Crucify him! We will not have this man to reign over us!" Instead of loyalty to Christ, across North America we hear the Beach Boys leading the masses in a worshipful "Maharishi, maharishi, maharishi" and almost a million TMers adulating over and over and over again, "Mantra, mantra, mantra."

Jude describes aptly how "false teachers carelessly go right on living their evil, immoral lives, degrading their bodies and laughing at those in authority over them, even scoffing at the Glorious Ones.... [they] mock and curse at anything they do not understand, and, like animals, they do whatever they feel like, thereby ruining their souls.... They are evil smears among you, laughing and carrying on, gorging and stuffing themselves without a thought for others. They are like clouds blowing over dry land without giving rain, promising much, but producing nothing. They are like fruit trees without any fruit at picking time. They are not only dead, but doubly dead, for they have been pulled out, roots and all, to be burned. All they leave behind them is shame and disgrace like the dirty foam left along the beach by the wild waves. They wander around looking as bright as stars, but ahead of them is the everlasting gloom and darkness that God has prepared for them" (Jude 8-10, 12, 13).

Another sign of the second coming of Jesus Christ is increasingly unrestrained immorality. "Miss Nude America," an outspoken witch and Satan worshiper, received her award before a crowd of several thousand and immediately announced her plans to parachute naked from an airplane before thousands of gazing spectators. A *New York Times* article (February 4, 1973) on satanism and sex reported that in "suburban basements around the country partners will peel off their clothes"; next comes "a visit with Satan himself ... intercourse with all the women ... followed by a general sexual free-for-all. In the old days," notes *The Times,* "the local officials of the inquisitions would descend upon you, but the Inquisition closed up shop some time ago, and most police forces have better things to do than to ride herd on the devil."

THE DEVIL

We turn to the *Time* magazine cover story entitled "Satan Returns" (June 19, 1972) and find that "all across the U. S. nowadays ... college-educated people gather in a house in a middle-class neighborhood, remove their clothes, and whirl through the double spiral of a witches' dance." In a typical meeting, notes *Time*, "the hour is midnight. On the front door of the house is an orange emblem showing black pitchforks. Downstairs the party is gathered solemnly before a black-draped altar. Facing them, on the wall, is a chartreuse goat-image superimposed on a purple pentagram. 'Tonight there is one among us elected to the priesthood of Mendes,' intones one of the men. 'Satan, thou hast seen fit to charge Warlock Shai with thy priesthood on earth ... the deification of the human race.' Reciting an ordination rite first in Latin and then in English, the speaker taps a second man on each shoulder with a sword. Someone pours flash powder on the sterno altar flame and whoosh! Fire leaps toward the ceiling." One would think he was reading about an ancient tribal ritual in some remote mud hut village. But it is a description of what is happening in "civilized" North America today.

Time states further that "the recrudescence of satanism in modern devil cults [is] the product of a playboy culture." Quoting sociologist Marcello Truzzi, *Time* observes that "satanism consists primarily of sex clubs that embellish their orgies with satanist rituals." It is significant that *Playboy* magazine would not have been allowed on our newsstands before the middle of this century. Today its circulation is one of the largest of any magazine in the Western world. A hundred other magazines far more daring and bold wholesale sex as a religion from Minneapolis to Melbourne, from Montreal to Munich. Some pagan religions, say in India or Central Africa,

have deified sex organs and sex orgies in their temples
for millennia. Now this demon-inspired worship has
come to America and is spreading like wildfire.

In mid-1976 a polling of North Americans
reported in the media that gazing at genitals is not
only a currently fashionable proclivity of males at
females but, in a new twist, of females at males. Bishop
Festo Kivengere of Central Africa stated that all this is
no more nor less than a veritable "trend toward the kind
of religion that most of my people were converted
from." The impact on society at large is heavy.
Quoting *Redbook* (September 1975), the *New York
Times* noted that whereas 33 percent of women in the
U. S. had had premarital relations in 1953 (The Kinsey
Report), by 1975 it was up to 80 to 90 percent for
women under twenty-five. Census reporters point out
the fact that the number of unwedded couples living
together has sky-rocketed by 700 percent in the last
fifteen years. The divorce rate has gone up another
6 percent in the last year in the United States; in
Canada it has quadrupled in the last decade.

All this reminds us of the truth of Max Lerner's
indictment that "America is now living a Babylonian
existence." John described a vision in which an angel
announced, "Babylon ... has become a den of
demons ... For all the nations have drunk the fatal
wine of her intense immorality" (Revelation 18:2, 3).
Ruth Graham has said that if God does not judge America
for her sins, he will have to apologize to Sodom and
Gomorrah.

Some people believe that John's revelation refers to
the Western world. Whether they are right, only
God knows. But there are some terrifying
similarities. The judgment of God is sure as we
approach the culmination of history with the second
coming of Jesus Christ. John wrote, "Her

THE DEVIL

businessmen were known around the world and she
deceived all nations with her sorceries" (Revelation
18:23). This can be compared to the current craze
for spiritism, voodoo, demon worship, and astrology
evidenced in our newspapers, magazines, pop song
lyrics, and novels. *(The Exorcist* has been one of the
decade's most popular books and movies.)

Further, "the world leaders, who took part in her
immoral acts and enjoyed her favors ... And all the
shipowners and captains of the ships and crews ...
[will say] 'she made us all rich from her great wealth.
And now in a single hour all is gone' " (Revelation 18:9,
17, 19). Gone because "her sins are piled as high as
heaven and God is ready to judge her for her crimes"
(18:5). Gone in what seems to a modern observer to be a
thermonuclear holocaust: "In a single day ... she shall
be utterly consumed by fire; for mighty is the Lord
who judges her" (18:8).

Actually the sins of rebellion and demon worship have
gone together since ancient times. The Hebrew
prophet and judge Samuel noted that "rebellion is as
bad as the sin of witchcraft" (1 Samuel 15:23). Avery
Brundage, long-time president of the International
Olympic Committee, said, "The rebellion of youth
today is worldwide." In addition, the drug pandemic is
raging in America and racing around the world. Because
of a reduction in "drugs as news," some have falsely
assumed that there has been a reduction of drug use. On
the contrary, *The New York Times* quotes the National
Institution of Drug Abuse as stating that again in the
mid-seventies, as in the sixties, there has been a
tragic "increase of all types of drugs."

For example, in two years the use of marijuana, either
in experimentation or on a regular basis, by fourteen-
and fifteen-year olds increased from 10 percent to
55 percent. Notes *The London Observer* in the

mid-seventies: "Drug abuse all over the world has assumed 'epidemic proportions.' " It goes on to note that according to reports submitted to the International Narcotics Board by national and regional authorities, the most "ominous change" for the worse has not only been in the escalating quantities of drugs being used throughout the world, but in "the recent tendency for abusive consumption to spread from single drugs to multi-drug abuse: 'the toxic affect of a given drug may be and often is greatly enhanced by consumption together with another drug.' "

The Bible states that Babylon "deceived all the nations with her sorceries" (Revelation 18:23). The word translated "sorceries" here is the Greek *pharmakeia,* which means "enchantment with drugs." The present preoccupation with drugs is a fulfillment of biblical prophecy. In June 1976 a coast to coast NBC-TV news special on transcendental meditation featured the fact that in the American youth culture, the heavy drugs era, and especially LSD, provided an open door through which Eastern guru-centered religions entered the West. NBC pointed especially to the 775,000 membership of the TM movement, with Hare Krishna and Maharaj Ji trailing not far behind.

Only five usages of the word *pharmakeia* (or related forms) occur in the New Testament. In Revelation 21:8 the word is used to identify those who are relegated to perdition: "Cowards who turn back from following me, and those who are unfaithful to me, and the corrupt, and murderers, and the immoral, and those conversing with demons [*pharmakeus*] and all liars—their doom is in the lake that burns with fire and sulphur." Then in Revelation 22:15, we read further of the inhabitants of hell: "those who have strayed away from God, and the sorcerers [*pharmakeia*—those

who have administered enchantment with drugs] and
the immoral and murderers and idolaters, and all who
love to lie, and do so.''

Paul warns that ''when you follow your own wrong
inclinations your lives will produce these evil results:
impure thoughts, eagerness for lustful pleasure,
idolatry, spiritism [*pharmakeia*] (that is,
encouraging the activity of demons)'' (Galatians
5:19, 20).

It has been said that history repeats itself. The
churches of Galatia, in the area of modern day Turkey,
were the only churches to which Paul wrote a warning
against ''enchantment with drugs.'' John wrote the
Revelation specifically to churches in a crescent of
seven cities, all of which are in modern Turkey.

With this in mind, think of where most of the heroin
used today comes from. According to a cover story in
Time (June 29, 1970) on world drug traffic, heroin has
''flowed from the poppy fields of Turkey [via] the labs
of Marseilles'' through the infamous ''French
connection,'' often by circuitous routes. The
American government took dramatic steps in the
early seventies to stop Turkey's farmers from
producing poppies, only to have this all reversed in the
mid-seventies when relations deteriorated because of
the war over Cyprus. The United States government
expenditure on drug control has been upped over 900
percent in the last five years in an attempt to cope
with heroin addiction, which has escalated 1,000
percent since 1960. Five billion dollars is now spent
annually on heroin in the United States: that's one in
every $300 of the gross national product. In New York
City, where there are a third of a million heroin addicts,
50 percent of all crime is related to drug addiction.
According to Joel Fort, M.D., in an article in a
national magazine, thefts by addicts from the general

population amount to 7.3 billion dollars annually.

The prospects for the future look grim. Most addicts used to be the inner-city poor. Now a large percentage are upper-income surburbanites. Even children are becoming involved in drugs. According to Dr. Fort, "Doctors are predicting a heroin epidemic, bringing us all together into a global drug village." The drug problem is seen in sports the world over, as reported by newspapers in connection with the Olympics. It's in industry. A news magazine quoted an industrial authority as lamenting of workers in Detroit's car lines, "Either they're taking pills to keep awake or they're zonked on a joint they had on a break."

It is hardly surprising then that a president of the United States went so far as to say: "The problem of narcotics trafficking and addiction is our number one domestic priority." To meet this challenge, massive manpower, brainpower, and other resources must be assembled to launch an all-out attack, he said, also declaring, "The war against narcotics is every bit as crucial as keeping out armed enemy invaders." Compare this with a prophecy of Isaiah: "When the enemy shall come in like a flood, the Spirit of the Lord shall lift up a standard against him" (59:19, KJV). Who is this enemy? The devil. What is one of his flood measures? Drugs. They can open people's minds to demons. The American Medical Association says in its official journal that drugs have now eclipsed mental retardation as the most prevalent affliction among the young. Dr. Paul H. Blachley of the University of Oregon Medical School states that experimentation has shown drug addiction to be a stronger drive than sex or hunger or thirst.

Can preventive measures stop the drugs craze? No. A recent report says that putting up posters in schools warning, "When Flower Children Go to Pot

They Become Blooming Idiots," "Bennies—Breakfast
of Chumpions," "Dope—It Takes One to Take
Some," or "Speed Kills! Don't 'Meth' Around,"
actually don't stop, or even slow the spread. It makes
kids giggle, not kick their habit.

The current drug scourge is not unique to North
America. The U.N. Secretary-General stated that it is a
"universal menace to which no country is immune."
Indeed it is spreading throughout the world with
alarming rapidity. Only one in ten of the world's drug
addicts is in the United States. Western Europeans
used to dismiss hard drugs as "an American
problem." But today, according to a government
official, they're becoming alarmed "about what the late
1970s will bring all over the world."

Figures from the communist world are not available.
Opium dealers in China are shot on sight, and we can
safely assume that drug abuse in Red China is very
much underground. But in the U.S.S.R., according
to a former Russian police operations officer who
defected to this country, drug abuse among "the young
people of Russia today is far, far worse than you would
ever read about in the free world. Our Russian young
people are cut loose [and turning to] drugs as a way of
escape."

Clearly the Bible indicates that by the time of
Christ's return, demon activity through "the
enchantment of drugs" will have risen above being
underground and illegal, and will be an institutionalized
lever of those who seize power, used to manipulate
and shape others. Already drugs are ingrained in the
fabric of the world's people in perhaps a much more
subtle way than most know. Dr. William Reilly,
writing in *The British Medical Journal* (October 1975)
notes that women car drivers in England who are
"pill-poppers" and "doped up dollies of the road" are

more and more becoming a major menace in today's traffic.

A U. S. senator wrote in a national magazine recently that if every source of illegally grown or manufactured drugs were cut off, the U. S. would scarcely feel any withdrawal symptoms, nor would the current drug-abuse epidemic be ended. The senator points out that "day after day, we're told by the 'electronic hypochondriac' [television] that drugs are an instant answer to whatever worries, annoys, or disturbs us." He said that no less than one billion dollars are being spent annually on breaking down our resistance to these chemical crutches.

The senator quotes Dr. Mitchell S. Rosenthal of New York City who said before a Senate hearing that "while everyone deplores the misuse of psychoactive drugs by young people, a major industry with practically unlimited access to the mass media has been convincing the American people, young and old alike, that drugs effect instant and significant changes, that they indeed work 'miracles.' "

"Miracles by drugs" ought to ring a familiar bell to a Bible believer. Paul wrote to the Thessalonians that the "man of sin will come as Satan's tool, full of satanic power, and will trick everyone with strange demonstrations, and will do great miracles" (2 Thessalonians 2:9).

Before we take a closer look at what the Bible says about the coming Antichrist, let us look at the fifth New Testament usage of the word *pharmakeia*, in Revelation 9:21. In the preceding verses, we read of the terrible unleashing of lethal forces: "the four mighty demons held bound at the great River Euphrates" are "turned loose to kill a third of all mankind. They led an army of 200,000,000 warriors—I heard an announcement of how many there were" (9:14-16).

"But the men left alive," John said in 9:20, 21,
"would not renounce their demon-worship ...
Neither did they change their mind and attitude about
all their murders and witchcraft" (pharmakeia—
"enchantment with drugs"). Drug-induced demon
possession will grip men. Though one-third of the
population of the earth is exterminated in one terrible
apocalyptic stroke, those remaining will not repent of
their "enchantment with drugs." Why? Because
the devil has overpowered them so completely that
they cannot retrieve themselves from his diabolical
hold.

This brings us back to the biblical statements—
which are too many for us to refer to adequately
here—regarding Satan and the Antichrist—allusions
which have a fascination for the public today as seen in
the film sensations *The Antichrist* and *The Omen*.
Paul told the Thessalonians that the "man of
rebellion [the Antichrist] will not come until the one
who is holding him back [the Holy Spirit] steps out of the
way ... Then there will be a time of great rebellion
against God, and then the man of rebellion will
come—the son of hell. He will defy every god there is,
and tear down every other object of adoration and
worship. He will go in and sit as God in the temple of
God, claiming that he himself is God." Paul added that
"this wicked one" when he arrives will show "great
miracles. He will completely fool those who are on
their way to hell because they have said 'no' to the
Truth; they have refused to believe it and love it, and
let it save them, so God will allow them to believe
lies with all their hearts, and all of them will be justly
judged for believing falsehood, refusing the Truth, and
enjoying their sins" (2 Thessalonians 2:7, 3, 4, 8-12).

A great deal has been written about the Antichrist in
the Bible and throughout history. *The New Catholic*

Encyclopedia (1966) states, "Catholic theologians
have been nearly unanimous in maintaining that the
Antichrist will be an individual person ... The Antichrist
is preserved for the 'last times.' His tyranny is to last
until Jesus Christ vanquishes him and sets up his
Kingdom on earth."

"False christs" and "many antichrists,"
according to the Bible, will precede the coming of *the*
Antichrist. Professor David L. Miller of Syracuse
University observes that it seems incredible that modern
man should suddenly shift to an obsessive "interest in
the occult, in magic, in extraterrestrial life, in Hindu
India and Buddhist Japan, in multi-demoned China, in
sorcery, in 'new religions' and many other meaning
systems hitherto foreign." Claiming to be Christ
today are such people as Charles Manson, Sun Myung
Moon, the "child" guru Maharaj Ji, and the Maharishi,
whose gathering of 30,000 new American converts
every month gets for him a *Time* cover story. Despite
his denials, reckons *Time* magazine, the Maharishi
does in fact claim to be a religious messiah.
Professor Ab Bharati says there are currently 2,000
"christs" in the U. S. Harvard professor Harvey Cox
labels this as "the age of instant gurus, when any nabob
with a half complacent public relations staff is assured
of a covey of Western devotees the moment he
announces his divinity." Certainly when Uri Geller
performs his inexplicable wonders on television,
when we read again of Charles Manson's capacity to
mesmerize his followers into worshipful and slavish
obedience, or for that matter, when we see the diplomatic
magic of a Henry Kissinger, we are seeing shadowy
harbingers of the future Antichrist.

All those people should not surprise us, for the Bible
predicts that the pressures of satanic influence will
build up prior to the coming of Christ in a multitude of

insidious ways. Most evident will be the appearance of false christs (Matthew 24:5) and "antichrists" (1 John 2:18, KJV). Satan will also embody himself in what the Bible calls "the beast" (Revelation 11:7; 13:1, 11; 15:2; 16:13; 17:8; 19:19; 20:10, KJV); the "False Prophet" (Revelation 20:10); and the "Antichrist" (1 John 2:18)—a trinity of evil. The devil will pretend to be the Father, the Antichrist will masquerade as the Son (he is the "son of perdition"), and the False Prophet will pose as the Holy Spirit. Is it any wonder that so many "messiahs" today exude "charisma"— precisely a precursor of what is to come!

John gave a graphic picture of this satanic manifestation in Revelation 13:1-4. "In my vision, I saw a strange Creature rising up out of the sea." ("Sea" in the Bible frequently refers figuratively to the masses of humanity.) The Devil "gave him his own power and throne and great authority." The Creature was "wounded beyond recovery—but the fatal wound was healed! All the world marveled at this miracle and followed the Creature in awe." Here is the devil aping God with a miraculous healing. So the peoples "worshiped the Dragon [Satan] for giving him such power and they worshiped the strange Creature. 'Where is there anyone as great as he?' they exclaimed. 'Who is able to fight against him?' "

How near man is to accepting such a leader today! Take, for example, the statement of the late Paul-Henri Spaak (1899-1972), the first president of the General Assembly of the United Nations, a founder of the Council of Europe, and a prophet and promulgator of the European Common Market. Said Dr. Spaak, "The truth is that the method of international committees has failed." And, "the highest order of experience" indicates that only a world ruler can control an otherwise fast disintegrating world. "Let him come,

and let him come quickly," "galvanize all
governments," and "vanquish" anarchy from the
earth. As the late Walter Lippmann once put it, the
world is more and more "ungoverned and
ungovernable." Professor Roy Fuller of Oxford
University says that he can see the handwriting on the
walls of both America and Europe—dictatorship is
beckoning. A European diplomat once said, "If the
devil will offer us a solution to our problems, then I
will follow the devil." What is tragic about a statement
like that is that this will become the prevailing attitude.

John tells us how the devil "encouraged the
Creature to speak great blasphemies against the Lord;
and gave him authority to control the earth for
forty-two months. All that time he blasphemed
God's Name and his temple and all those living in
heaven. The Dragon [Satan] gave him power to fight
against God's people and to overcome them, and to rule
over all nations and language groups throughout the
world. And all mankind—whose names were not
written down before the founding of the world in the
slain Lamb's Book of Life—worshiped the evil
Creature." John goes on to declare that the
Antichrist will do "unbelievable miracles such as
making fire flame down to earth from the skies while
everyone was watching. By doing these miracles, he
was deceiving people everywhere. He could do these
marvelous things," and many others. But he would
demand absolute allegiance and obedience as "he
required everyone—great and small, rich and poor,
slave and free—to be tattooed with a certain mark on
the right hand or on the forehead. And no one could get a
job or even buy in any store without the permit of that
mark, which was either the name of the Creature or the
code number of his name."

This is all found in Revelation 13:5-17. It almost

reads like a passage from George Orwell's *1984*.
Today, with *1984* becoming nearer reality, the world
seems to be helplessly drawn toward totalitarianism. In
mid-1976, Freedom House, the U. S. eclectic
watchdog of democracy, claims that the percentage of
the world's population which lives under democracy
has been reduced over the last three years from 61
percent to 19 percent. The Bible prophesies that a
dictatorship will take over the world. The dictator will
be Antichrist.

Everywhere today man talks of "peace, peace; when
there is no peace" (Jeremiah 8:11, KJV). The Bible
also predicts that both "priests and prophets give
assurances of peace when all is war" (Jeremiah 6:14).
Even at the first World Congress of Witchcraft in
1975, it was announced that plans were being made to
get the psychics of Russia and other trouble spots in the
world together for the purpose of "preventing World War
III."

People are desperate for peace. In fact, one of the
first acts of the Antichrist will be to sign a peace pact
with Israel. The Bible clearly predicts that this
peace pact will be broken, and that after this will
come one final war—Armageddon. Today blocs of
nations are forming for that terrible apocalyptic
showdown. It is the devil's masterpiece. By this time,
he will have displayed "miracle-working demons [who]
conferred with all the rulers of the world to gather
them for battle against the Lord on that great
coming Judgment Day of God Almighty ... And they
gathered all the armies of the world near a place called,
in Hebrew, Armageddon" (Revelation 16:14, 16).

Note that the Bible says that *the devil will be
responsible for bringing the nations of the world to
Armageddon.*

How close is Armageddon? The Bible tells us

neither to set a date nor name an hour in which "the end of the age" will come. But it does give us many signs which will signal the coming again of Jesus Christ and the end of the age.

Already the beginnings of the violence of that catastrophic time of "great tribulation" (Matthew 24:21; Revelation 2:22, KJV) seem to be gathering momentum. The devil has always been a warmonger and instigator of violence. Today's world seems to be riddled with men in whom Satan is stirring up violence of the most vicious sort. Twenty years ago who would have foreseen today's anti-hijacking devices in our airports, resembling wartime measures? In 1972 a Delta Airlines jet was commandeered by a Detroit family to Algeria with a record-breaking million dollar ransom on board. In the hijackers' home, the police "found a mound of earth, food which apparently was offered to pagan gods, and a white plastic doll with a knife stuck in it."

We pick up our newspapers, listen to our radios, and watch the news on TV during any week, and learn of violence on an unbelievable scale. In Montreal, two men get drunk and are rejected from a club. So they force their way back in with a fire bomb and blow up the place, killing thirty-seven people. In Chicago twenty-seven murders are committed in one weekend. Thousands of people in an African country are ruthlessly slaughtered during the course of a few weeks. Angola, Rhodesia, Lebanon, South Africa—all are symbols of millions of volcanos erupting, of violence incarnate! It seems that the entire earth is being enveloped in flames of spreading terror: omens of Armageddon, with Linus Pauling, the Nobel Prize winner, reckoning that up ahead there will be as much suffering in a year or two as during whole previous centuries of human history.

THE DEVIL

An editor of *The Toronto Globe and Mail* stated, "In today's weird world there seems to exist a climate in which violence can breed like some evil growth in a hothouse. Just a few seeds, sprinkled here and there, quickly take root and grow into plants of utter horror. Is all of this just some irreversible malady of the times, before which we all stand mute and terrified until it has run its course?" The tragic answer is Yes. It is the devil on the march. He is mobilizing his demonic denizens in a final effort to take over the world and place all human inhabitants under his direct tyranny.

Meanwhile, those of us who are believers in Jesus Christ as Lord are looking, not for the second coming of Satan, but for the return of the Lord Jesus Christ and our consequent deliverance forever from the assaults of the devil. Paul wrote to the Thessalonians that one day "the Lord himself will come down from heaven with a mighty shout and with the soul-stirring cry of the archangel and the great trumpet-call of God. And the believers who are dead will be the first to rise to meet the Lord. Then we who are still alive and remain on the earth will be caught up with them in the clouds to meet the Lord in the air and remain with him forever. So comfort and encourage each other with this news" (1 Thessalonians 4:16-18).

CHAPTER TWO

Before There Was a Devil

The seventeenth-century poet John Donne wrote that two things he could not fathom: "Where all the past years are, and who cleft the devil's foot." The origin, existence, and activities of the devil have always been among man's most puzzling problems.

Pope Paul VI reckons that anyone who currently rejects the existence of a personal devil has to consider evil as some kind of "pseudoreality, a conceptual and fanciful personification of the unknown causes of our misfortunes. The problem of evil seen in its complexity and in its absurdity from the viewpoint of our one-sided rationality becomes an obsession. It's the greatest difficulty for our religious understanding of the cosmos."

C. S. Lewis prefaced *The Screwtape Letters* with an expression of his understanding of who the devil is: "The commonest question is whether I really 'believe in the devil.' Now, if by 'the devil' you mean a power opposite to God and, like God, self-existent from all eternity, the answer is certainly no. There is no uncreated being except God. God has no opposite. No being could attain a 'perfect badness' opposite to the perfect goodness of God. Satan, the leader or dictator of devils, is the opposite not of God, but of Michael.'' Lewis believed the devil was in that order of created beings which we know as angels.

Nowhere in the Bible do we read of God—Father, Son, or Holy Spirit—being created. God always, was, is, and always shall be: the eternal Deity, Trinity, Absolute Sovereign, Perfect Virtue. He is eternally perfect and unique. As Son of God, Jesus Christ was, and is, coexistent with God the Father and God the Holy Spirit.

Jesus, while he was here on earth, said one day to his disciples, ''I saw Satan falling from heaven as a flash of lightning!'' (Luke 10:18). Satan, before he was the devil and as such, the personification of evil, was Lucifer, a being created perfect: ''You were perfect in all you did from the day you were created'' (Ezekiel 28:15). Lucifer's holiness (28:18) was one of his original characteristics; he was morally sound. How long his integrity and allegiance to God lasted, we do not know. It would appear that for a period too long for our finite minds to fathom, he was a trusted and obedient lieutenant of the Almighty.

Lucifer was not only upright, but he was beautiful. The prophet Ezekiel described him: ''The Lord God says: You were the perfection of wisdom and beauty. You were in Eden, the garden of God; your clothing was bejeweled with every precious stone—ruby, topaz, diamond, chrysolite, onyx, jasper, sapphire, carbuncle, and emerald—all in beautiful settings of finest gold. They were given to you on the day you were created'' (28:12, 13).

Lucifer was also brilliant. "The Lord God says: You were the perfection of wisdom" (28:12). His wisdom was evidently not as valued by him as his beauty: "You corrupted your wisdom for the sake of your splendor" (28:17). Nevertheless, Lucifer had immense knowledge.

Moral, attractive, and wise, Lucifer also had immense power. "You were perfect in all you did from the day you were created" (28:15). Though Satan is not, and never has been, omnipotent (all-powerful), omniscient (all-knowing), or omnipresent (everywhere at once), Ezekiel points out that even in his pre-fallen state, Lucifer had an enormous capacity for achievement. The prophet observed that as a performer, Lucifer was a precisionist of the highest order among created beings.

Upright, beautiful, brilliant, and one who could get things done, God entrusted the highest of all offices in his interstellar universe to Lucifer. He says, "I appointed you to be the anointed guardian cherub. You had access to the holy mountain of God ... O overshadowing cherub" (28:14, 16). Lucifer, until his crash, had more power than any other created being throughout the universe.

Lucifer was the head of all the angels when he was toppled. The Apostle Paul, writing to the Ephesians, indicated that there is a hierarchy in God's angelic order: official graduations or ranks of angels identified by the categories "principality," "power," "might," and "dominion" (Ephesians 1:21, KJV). Lucifer was never the commander-in-chief of the angelic army, but he was a five-star general. It was when he aspired to be commander-in-chief that he came crashing down.

The idea of many levels of personalities in the universe is gaining more acceptance among scientists and scholars today. The Russians state candidly that their space scientists and astronomers are looking for evidence of life in outer space; they are starting from the premise that there is life. This is true of a great number of North American astrophysicists and other scholars. Says Professor Arthur Gibson of the University of Toronto, "I'd be appalled if there weren't hundreds of kinds of intelligences in the universe, both in our atmosphere and on other planets. Angels would be one example." Dr. Engstrom, a scientist and president of R.C.A., concurs, being convinced that the universe is not empty, but full of life.

The current interest in celestial or extraterrestrial life is evidenced by the popularity of books such as *Gods from Outer Space* and *Chariot of the Gods* by Erich Von Däniken, and *Worlds in Collision* and *Worlds in Upheaval* by Immanuel Velikofsky. Most people are aware of the constant flow of films about life in space, such as *The Outer Space Connection*, released in November 1975.

The Bible often refers to the vast number of living beings in space as angels. While a study of the characteristics and attributes of angels as they apply to the person of Satan and his demon kingdom belongs in the next chapter, it is relevant here to note that angels are the administrative branch in the government of God. They were created for a variety of functions, as indicated in the Word of God. They are "spirit-messengers sent out to help and care for those who are to receive his salvation" (Hebrews 1:14). Wrote the psalmist, "He orders his angels to protect you wherever you go. They will steady you with their hands to keep you from stumbling against the rocks on the trail" (Psalm 91:11, 12). So might we think of an unfallen Lucifer.

Angels also administer the fiats of God's Judgment— just as they did in Egypt when God sent judgment

on Pharoah and his hosts for refusing to release
Israel from bondage. So Lucifer, before his fall,
seems to have helped police the universe, as now he
patrols the earth (Job 1:7).

Angels were ambassadors of God's revelation, the
Word of God to man. The writer of Hebrews noted,
"The messages from angels have always proved true
and people have always been punished for
disobeying them" (2:2). So we might think of Lucifer
as a communications genius.

These are just a few of the functions angels perform,
but they indicate what Satan's official duties might
have been before he fell.

In the hierarchy of angels, the seraphim were the
second highest rank among angels in the universe;
the highest rank were the cherubim. Since Satan was
once the highest of the cherubim, we should see what
the Scriptures say about these creative beings.

Cherubim seem to vindicate God's holiness. After
God ejected Adam and Eve from the Garden of Eden,
"he placed at the east of the garden of Eden cherubim,
and a flaming sword which turned every way, to
keep the way of the tree of life" (Genesis 3:24, KJV).

God instructed Moses to place two solid gold images
of cherubim on the lid of the Ark of the Covenant, which
was to be placed in the Holy of Holies in the
Tabernacle. The Lord then promised Moses, "I will
meet with you there and talk with you from above the
place of mercy between the cherubim; and the Ark
will contain the laws of my covenant. There I will tell
you my commandments for the people of Israel"
(Exodus 25:22). God met Moses only when the
conditions of his holiness were met at the mercy seat,
where the lid covering the Ten Commandments was
guarded by the images of the cherubim.

The prophet Ezekiel saw, in a vision from God,

"a throne of beautiful blue sapphire [which]
appeared in the sky above the heads of the cherubim"
(Ezekiel 10:1). Here, in what has been considered one of
the most awe-inspiring chapters of the Bible, Ezekiel
describes how the cherubim cleansed with coals of fire
those who would approach God, thus vindicating the
character of the Almighty.

The Apostle John, caught up in a vision to heaven, sees
these same "Living Beings." He described their
activity: "Day after day and night after night they kept
on saying, 'Holy, holy, holy, Lord God Almighty—the
one who was, and is, and is to come.' And when the
Living Beings gave glory and honor and thanks to the
one sitting on the throne, who lives forever and ever,
the twenty-four Elders fell down before him and
worshiped him, the Eternal Living One, and cast their
crowns before the throne, singing, 'O Lord, you are
worthy to receive the glory and the honor and the
power, for you created all things. They were
created and called into being by your act of will' "
(Revelation 4:8-11).

Why all this attention to the cherubim? Because God
had said to Lucifer, "I appointed you to be the
anointed guardian cherub. You had access to the holy
mountain of God. You walked among the stones of
fire" (Ezekiel 28:14). But then, after much true and
pure sailing, Lucifer, a creature subject to the
Creator, decided to lead a revolt. His beauty had
inflated him with pride. He had incalculable knowledge;
but his wisdom was too small to keep him in the
balance of knowing and maintaining his place of
subordination to God. He had untold wealth, but he
lusted for more; he wanted to own and operate
everything. But God will not be overthrown.

Ezekiel described how God investigated the defiant
irregularities in his highest angel's conduct and

character. "You were perfect in all you did from the day you were created," God said, "until that time when wrong was found in you. Your great wealth filled you with internal turmoil and you sinned. Therefore, I cast you out of the mountain of God like a common sinner. I destroyed you, O overshadowing cherub, from the midst of the stones of fire. Your heart was filled with pride because of all your beauty; you corrupted your wisdom for the sake of your splendor. Therefore I have cast you down to the ground and exposed you helpless before the curious gaze of kings. You defiled your holiness with lust for gain; therefore I brought forth fire from your own actions and let it burn you to ashes upon the earth in the sight of all those watching you. All who know you are appalled at your fate; you are an example of horror; you are destroyed forever" (Ezekiel 28:15-19). Lucifer had sold out to sin and there was no redemption for him, ever.

If Ezekiel describes the *why* of Lucifer's judgment and damnation, Isaiah gives us the *how*. He points out Lucifer's five distinct "I will" resolutions which were unprecedented in their defiance. They threatened to bring about the total disintegration of the universe if God did not step in with immediate and eternal judgment.

Isaiah writes, "How you are fallen from heaven, O Lucifer, son of the morning! How you are cut down to the ground—mighty though you were ... For you said to yourself, 'I will ascend to heaven and rule the angels. I will take the highest throne. I will preside on the Mount of Assembly far away in the north. I will climb to the highest heavens and be like the Most High'" (14:12-14). Lucifer was not content to be the chief administrator of all created beings. He wanted to seize the reins of universal government. He wanted to be sovereign. He wanted to have absolute rule. He wanted to be God.

God said, "But instead, you will be brought down to the pit of hell, down to its lowest depth. Everyone there will stare at you and ask, 'Can this be the one who shook the earth and the kingdoms of the world? Can this be the one who destroyed the world and made it into a shambles...?' " (Isaiah 14:15-17).

This is the fall from heaven that Jesus told his disciples he himself had witnessed (Luke 10:18). Lucifer's tumble, some Bible scholars and students believe, left a pre-Adamic earth as a "shapeless, chaotic mass with the Spirit of God brooding over the dark vapors" (Genesis 1:2). This darkest moment in the history of the universe has been imaginatively described by many of the great literary writers, but never better than by John Milton in *Paradise Lost*.

A question immediately arises: Did Satan go down alone? The answer is a clear no. Satan took with him a colossal number of angels. Pope Paul once said, "It is not a question of one devil but of many [as] indicated by various passages in the Gospel." These fallen angels form a huge kingdom of demons who, once "creatures of God, but fallen, because of their rebellion and damnation," now constitute "a whole mysterious world."

Some people ask, "How could angels be so stupid as to join a mutiny against God?" I suggest that it was the same sort of thing which makes people today sympathize more with a criminal than with the criminal's victim. It was, perhaps, as the Rolling Stones sing, "Sympathy for the devil." Even Shakespeare, curiously enough, wrote, "Angels are bright still, though the brightest fell" (Macbeth, IV, iii, 22).

The number of the angels, fallen and unfallen, is unknown. The writer to the Hebrews referred to an "innumerable company of angels" (Hebrews 12:22, KJV). We can assume that the number of demons, even though a fraction of the original number of angels, is astronomical.

Lucifer's insurrection was the greatest ever! When he was demoted by God, he must have lobbied relentlessly among the angels. Long before he talked Eve into responding to temptation, he cajoled angels in doing so. On the other hand, these angels were responsible for their own sin. Jude pointed out: "I remind you of those angels who were once pure and holy, but turned to a life of sin" (vs. 6). They "abandoned their original rank and left their proper home," says the *Living Bible* footnote giving an alternate translation for this verse.

Satan is an absolute dictator over these fallen angels, the demons and evil spirits prowling the earth and seeking to possess the earth's inhabitants. The devil is constantly at work as "the king of demons" (Luke 11:15). Satan evidently delegates this demon army to perform specified tasks. A master economist as well as a strategist, he could depute many demons to occupy one man. When Jesus asked the demoniac of Gadara, "What is your name?" the demons answered, "Legion" (Luke 8:30). If the demons were telling the truth, the man was controlled by thousands of demons. (A Roman army legion consisted of 6,000 troops.)

It is little wonder, then, that Paul warned the Ephesian believers that our warfare is spiritual; we battle "persons without bodies—the evil rulers of the unseen world, those mighty satanic beings and great evil princes of darkness who rule this world" (Ephesians 6:12), who use "all strategies and tricks of Satan" (6:11). How could they do this with such precision and potency if they were not under the direct control of Satan?

THE DEVIL

One of Satan's "tricks" is to exploit the grief of a bereaved person by sending an evil spirit to impersonate the deceased, purporting to have a message for the bereaved. Several years ago, Bishop Pike fell into this trap. Today an Oscar-winning actress (whose mother, an equally famous actress, committed suicide) is saying, "My mother's ghost guides my career."

Is it any wonder that our world is in the mess it's in today? One of America's founding fathers observed that if men will not be governed by God, then they will be ruled by tyrants. The devil is a tyrant. Only with God's help can men and women "escape from Satan's trap of slavery to sin which he uses to catch them whenever he likes" (2 Timothy 2:26). This could scarcely be otherwise when Satan has evil princes so immediately at his command.

The fact that most people seem to be ignorant of Satan and his network does not mean that he does not exist. One reason why people shun the truth about Satan is that it is admittedly the most tragic story ever told, not merely because he himself tumbled from the heights of the universe, but because of the millions of beings he took with him and the consequent havoc they work on the human race.

Perhaps the chief lesson we can learn from our biblical investigation into the devil's beginnings is the lesson the British Admiral Viscount Horatio Nelson learned at Trafalgar in 1805. "Never underestimate your enemy!" counseled Nelson. The Bible tells us never to underestimate the power of the devil.

A friend of mine has recently served as president of the American Baptist Convention. He is a scholar, pastor of a large congregation, with many social services connected to his ministry. He was recently walking along one of the hallways of his church when, he is convinced, he encountered the devil, who accosted him physically and threw him to the floor.

According to *The New York Times,* "Msgr. Luigi Novarase, the official exorcist of the diocese of Rome, is quite convinced that he has done battle with the devil."

Martin Luther one day was so convinced that he was face-to-face with the devil that he threw an inkwell at him. Expressing his encounters with Satan in perhaps the foremost of modern hymns, "A Mighty Fortress Is Our God," Luther set the Reformation world to singing:

> And tho' this world, with devils filled,
> Should threaten to undo us,
> We will not fear, for God hath willed
> His truth to triumph through us:
> The Prince of Darkness grim—we tremble not for
>   him;
> His rage we can endure,
> For lo, his doom is sure,
> One little word shall fell him.

CHAPTER THREE

Meet Your Enemy

The reality of Satan is clearly taught in the Scriptures. He is not a medieval spook or goblin. He is not a nebulous negative influence of some kind. He is not a sort of scapegoat on whom one can conveniently heap his hangups. He is not a metaphorical whipping post to absorb the blame for all our accumulated human woes. Nor are the devil and evil synonymous. Indeed the devil is evil, as God is good. But this does not mean that the devil is an abstraction— he is a person.

Pope Paul is right in insisting that "whoever refuses to acknowledge [a personal devil's] existence is beyond the pale of biblical or ecclesiastical teachings." Similarly, a recent United Presbyterian Church Commission report (USA) affirms that all attempts by the intellectually oriented zealots within the church to demythologize the idea of a personal devil "have been vain attempts to escape from the evil reality of man's adversary, an antichrist devil." The report also affirms that "no man who has looked long and hard at the intractable abysmal depth of human iniquity can deny" that there is a person behind it all, a person the Bible calls Satan.

In his letter to the Ephesians, the Apostle Paul clearly identified the devil and his demons as "persons." He said, "Put on all of God's armor ... For we are not fighting against people made of flesh and blood, but against persons without bodies ... those mighty satanic beings ... huge numbers of wicked spirits in the spirit world" (Ephesians 6:11, 12). Not only does the Bible teach that the devil and his demons are persons, but it teaches that they are angels. John said the devil is "the angel of the bottomless pit" (Revelation 9:11, KJV). Hell is prepared for "the devil and his angels" (Matthew 25:41, KJV).

Since Satan is an angel, and all his evil spirits are angels, it is important to note some of the characteristics of angels. Only by so doing can we understand the personality, power, and limitations of Satan and his kingdom of demons.

The character of an unfallen angel differs dramatically from that of an angel who has forfeited his integrity in order to follow Satan. But the basic nature, features, and capacities of all angels are comparable, just as the nature, features, and capacities of all men are essentially the same, though their character, conduct, and destiny differ radically.

In the order of his creation, God placed the angels higher than man. We read in Hebrews that when the Son of God became man (compare John 1:14), he did not take on him the nature of angels, but became "a little lower than the angels" (2:9, KJV). This does not, of course, imply that Christ, both before the

Incarnation and after, has not utilized an angelic body
to appear to man in a form which theologians call
"Christophany."

Jesus made it clear that angels are sexless
(Matthew 22:30), so we can assume that their number
is fixed. They are capable of sin, and their sin is
apparently unpardonable (Jude 6). Angels are
corruptible, but they are indestructible. Each angel is
immortal (Luke 20:36).

Paul wrote to the Corinthians that "the angels in
heaven have bodies far different from ours," but
nonetheless, "bodies." A little later he said, "just as
there are natural, human bodies, there are also
supernatural, spiritual bodies." Paul also pointed out that
the celestial bodies are not subject, as "our earthly
bodies," to death and decay (1 Corinthians 15:40, 44,
42).

Though angels were created higher than man,
they can appear to man. Throughout the Bible
angels, unfallen and fallen, appeared to people—as
people. They sometimes appeared in dreams, as they did
to Joseph (Matthew 1:20; 2:13, 19); or in visions, as
they did to John (see The Revelation). They appeared in
bodily form, as they did to Paul (Acts 27:23) and Peter
(Acts 12:7-9). Sometimes they were dressed in
brilliant white, so clothed with the glory of the Lord
that they were simply overpowering (Matthew 28:2-4;
Luke 2:9; Acts 1:10). They might even be multiwinged
(Isaiah 6:2) or appear among whirling wheels of
magnificent splendor (Ezekiel 10).

But having said that, we must add that the Scriptures
often appeared quite indistinguishable from human beings. Those they visited often thought they were being
visited by a man. The writer to the Hebrews exhorted,
"Don't forget to be kind to strangers, for some who
have done this have entertained angels without

THE DEVIL

realizing it'' (Hebrews 13:2).

When the prophet Daniel was thrown to the lions, an angel came to shut the lions' mouths (Daniel 6:22). Later we read the account of how the prophet met the angel Gabriel (8:17-27; 9:21-27) and perhaps Michael (10:13). He found it so difficult to identify the angel that he wrote, "Then someone—he looked like a man—touched my lips.... Then the one who seemed to be a man touched me again, and I felt my strength returning. 'God loves you very much,' he said, 'don't be afraid!' '' (10:16, 18, 19). Then Daniel realized that he was indeed an angel come to tell him what was "written in the 'Book of the Future' '' (10:20).

In Judges, we read of how the Angel of the Lord appeared to the barren wife of Manoah, to promise her the birth of a son, Samson. She ran to tell her husband, "A man from God appeared to me." Manoah didn't yet realize that he was the Angel of the Lord (13:2-16). "The Angel of the Lord," many believe, was Christ himself appearing in an angelic body.

Another instance happened earlier. Gideon was a farmer, and it was threshing time. "One day the Angel of the Lord came and sat beneath the oak tree at Ophrah." He said to Gideon, "Mighty soldier, the Lord is with you!" Gideon replied, "Stranger, if the Lord is with us, why has all this happened to us?" After a considerable discussion and the first of several miracles it took to convince Gideon that he was being called of God, Gideon finally "realized that it had indeed been the Angel of the Lord" (Judges 6:11-22).

These were typical reactions to the personal appearances of angels. In fact, Jacob wrestled with a Man at Peniel through the second half of a night and ended up with a dislocated hip. His name was changed from Jacob to Israel. And for his faithfulness in the conflict, he was awarded a special blessing from the Lord (Genesis 32:24-30). We know the Man was an angel from Hosea 12:4 where the prophet states that Jacob wrestled with the "Angel."

Angels have names. Jacob asked the Angel, "What is your name?" The Angel replied, "You mustn't ask" (Genesis 32:29). Manoah "asked him [the Angel] for his name," and once again the reaction: " 'Don't even ask my name,' the Angel replied, 'for it is a secret' " (Judges 13:17, 18). Jesus asked the maniac of Gadara, "What is your name?... The demon replied, 'Legion, for there are many of us here within this man' " (Mark 5:9). Angels, whether fallen (demons) or unfallen, all seem to have names, although it is with the utmost reluctance they divulge this information to men.

Angels are capable of many "human" activities. They can be visible to man, as we have already noted. They can be seen by animals (Numbers 22:23). They can look so much like men that corrupt people, like those who lived in Sodom, can find them sexually attractive (Genesis 19:1-11). Angels can eat a meal (Genesis 19:3; see also Hebrews 13:2); they also have their own special delicate food (Psalm 78:25). They have tremendous strength—they can do such things as roll away a huge stone (Matthew 28:2), undo chains (Acts 12:7); or open prison gates (Acts 12:10). They can pull a threatened man through a door and lock out would-be intruders, temporarily blinding them (Genesis 19:10, 11). They can awaken a man and feed him (1 Kings 19:5). They can close lions' mouths (Daniel 6:22).

Angels can desire (1 Peter 1:12). They compliment (Judges 6:12). They are happy when sinners repent (Luke 15:10). They will bring judgment (Matthew 13:39, 49), but they will not control the future world (Hebrews 2:5). They can mobilize as a mighty army

(Matthew 26:53). They can kill an individual (Acts 12:23) or a multitude of people (2 Kings 19:35). On the other hand, two angels came to tell Lot to take his family and leave Sodom before they destroyed that city and Gomorrah (Genesis 19:1-29). An angel can effect the complete physical healing of a human being (John 5:4).

Angels have finite intelligence—they don't know everything. Indeed, they can make mistakes (Job 4:18). They can discern good and bad (2 Samuel 14:17). An unfallen angel will refuse to be worshiped (Revelation 22:8, 9); a fallen one will crave to be worshiped (Luke 4:6, 7).

Some of us have heard people tell how angels have appeared to them, but I give a note of caution. We should neither be too quick nor too slow to credit these accounts. In 1 Kings 13:11-26, we read how God had commissioned a prophet to perform a mission. Another elderly prophet heard about it and intercepted him with the words, "I am a prophet too, just as you are; and an angel gave me a message from the Lord. I am to take you home with me and give you food and water," which he did. But "the old man was lying to him," and the disobedient young prophet, because he took the word of another prophet above the Word of God, was slain by a lion as he went out again onto the road.

Paul was so emphatic about using discernment that he wrote to the Galatians, "Let God's curses fall on anyone, including myself, who preaches any other way to be saved than the one we told you about; yes, if an angel comes from heaven and preaches any other message, let him be forever cursed. I will say it again: if anyone preaches any other Gospel than the one you welcomed, let God's curse fall upon him" (Galatians 1:8, 9). Paul explained to the Corinthians why he would

not take a message from an angel without any
questioning: "Satan can change himself into an angel of
light" (2 Corinthians 11:14).

God may, however, in very special
circumstances today, send an angel to communicate
his will. One example is an experience of the late Dr. V.
Raymond Edman, whom I came to know and respect as
president of Wheaton College when I was a student
there, and also as chairman of our Billy Graham Team
Committee. Before going to Wheaton, Dr. and Mrs.
Edman were missionaries to Ecuador. There he
contracted a tropical disease and was so close to
death that his coffin had been made, and Mrs. Edman's
wedding dress had been dyed black in preparation for the
funeral. But in answer to prayer, Dr. Edman was
restored to health.

Such was their trial, however, that they were almost
down to their last dollar and they did not know what
to do. One day at noon, a peasant appeared on the
doorstep and clapped his hands, which is an equivalent
to our knocking on the door. In colloquial Spanish he
asked for the *Patron* (head of the household). He was
ushered in, and Dr. Edman came and received him. The
peasant then presented a gift of money, which was the
exact amount the Edmans needed and had prayed
for. Then he went as quietly as he had come.

Dr. Edman, a precise and thoughtful man, inquired
throughout the whole village as to who this person might
be. Not only could he find no clue to his identity, but
not one person had seen him come or go, which at high
noon in a village like that seemed impossible. Dr.
Edman was convinced that that day they had met an
angel.

We have noted that angels can appear in bodily form.
But let me ask this. Have most of us heard angels talk to
us, felt their hands touching us, or have we seen them?

The answer is No. Yet, because the Bible tells us so, we know that they help and care for all believers (Psalm 34:7; Hebrews 1:14).

The devil himself can also appear as a man. According to the Bible, Jesus went "out into the barren wastelands of Judea, where Satan tempted him for forty days" (Luke 4:1). There is no reason to believe that he appeared other than in a body, for "the angels ... have bodies" (1 Corinthians 15:40). The same would apply to Zechariah 3:1, where we are introduced to "Joshua the high priest standing before the angel of the Lord, and Satan standing at his right hand to resist him" (KJV). Consider also the case of King David taking a census of Israel. We read that "Satan stood up against Israel, and provoked David to number Israel. And David said to Joab and to the rulers of the people, 'Go, number Israel from Beersheba even to Dan' " (1 Chronicles 21:1, 2, KJV). Here again, the devil seems to have come in person to David and challenged him. And in addition to Satan himself coming in person as an angel, we read that there were occasions when God allowed "evil angels among [men]" (Psalm 78:49, KJV).

Feodor Dostoyevsky, in his portrayal of Satan visiting Ivan Karamazov, had him very much "a gentleman, or rather a peculiarly Russian sort of gentleman ... He looked like one of those landed proprietors who flourished during the days of serfdom." Dr. A. M. Greeley of the University of Chicago wrote in *The New York Times* (February 4, 1973) that he thinks of Satan incarnate as "the devil occupying a position as tenured faculty member at a divinity school in the San Francisco Bay area—probably specializing in the theology of revolution."

Vance Havner, a well-known evangelical preacher, once said that if the devil comes to town in a body, you won't likely find him in a nightclub or a gambling dive. The world and the flesh will look after these places. You'll more likely find him in a pulpit, with a D. D., drawing a salary for denying his own existence.

Although Satan and his angels have the capacity to appear in bodily form to men, they seem to prefer to attack people as spirits. They assault people from without, or actually enter into them.

We see throughout the Bible, and particularly in the New Testament, that Satan deputes his demons as spirits to enter into men, women, and children.

Because we depend so heavily on our five physical senses, it is easier to believe in angels who appear bodily than to believe in angels who never physically appear or speak to us. This is a natural reaction. It is like the battery in your car. If it's dead, the starter will not work, the lights will not go on, the horn will not blow, the automatic windows will not go down or up, and the heater or air conditioner fan will not turn. It is much easier to believe in the existence of the battery than in the electricity. But the electricity is no less real than the battery itself. As Christians, we know the importance of believing not only what we can see, but what we can't see, including the existence of God's and Satan's spirit armies.

No book or periodical can match the Scriptures in the description of terrestrial and even interstellar scenes involving the angelic creation. If you want the drama of space-traveling beings with wings, it is to be found in Isaiah 6. If you want to read of wheel arrangements complicated enough to make the most modern differential or gearbox look like two pulleys joined by a belt, turn to Ezekiel 10. If you want to see angels so powerful that they can stand on the four corners of a charted earth, "holding back the four

THE DEVIL

winds," turn to Revelation 7:1. Or if you want to learn of ones so stupendous they can stand suspended visibly in the sky, "standing in the sunshine," turn to Revelation 19:17. The books of Revelation, Isaiah, Daniel, Ezekiel, and Zechariah speak of phenomena so beautiful that no tongue or pen on earth could adequately describe them and so horrifying that they would terrify man's most courageous heroes.

So angelic creation can appear disarmingly similar to ordinary human beings, or they can be overpoweringly extraterrestrial. The vehicle of communication with men can be physical or spiritual, sensory or extrasensory, depending on the circumstances and the nature of the message. But for the purposes of our observations here, we need to keep two things in mind: that the devil and all demons are angels; that under most circumstances the devil and his demons accost men as spirits.

The devil will come to man, as Pope Paul puts it, as "a living spiritual being, perverted and perverting. A terrible reality, mysterious and frightening." This is to the devil's advantage, because he wants men to be ignorant of the force which makes them act, think, and aspire to things which are irrational, illogical, and result only in destruction. As C. S. Lewis put it, "The devil that you can't see is worse than the devil that you can see." No one subscribes to that belief more consistently, in all but the most extraordinary of circumstances, than the devil himself.

There is an important point to note here. Satan occasionally does his evil work himself, but only when it is of prime or strategic importance. That Satan has always picked his own priorities is very clear from a study of the Scriptures. While from the dawn of history he has delegated most of his dirty work to his massive army of demons, he has consistently been present in person to perform the tasks which to him have been crucial.

But however menacing and threatening the devil and his angels may be, they are subject to the sovereignty of Jesus Christ and therefore can never make a move without his all-seeing, all-knowing, all-powerful Presence. So let us always keep in mind that while Satan is an angel, like all other angels he was made by Jesus Christ and is subject to him.

CHAPTER FOUR

Tragedy in Paradise

Adam had hardly carried Eve over the threshold when super-salesman Satan was on the doorstep, dressed in his Sunday best, hell-bent for the grandest larceny of all time. He was determined to turn the greatest tragedy of eternity, his own fall, into the greatest tragedy of time, the descent of man into sin. And he would succeed. Wrote Paul to the Romans, "When Adam sinned, sin entered the entire human race. His sin spread death throughout all the world, so everything began to grow old and die, for all sinned. We know that it was Adam's sin that caused this" (Romans 5:12, 13).

The whole direction of history was determined by what happened in the Garden of Eden. No social scientist, historian, philosopher, or theologian can fully understand man—what he is, where he came from, or where by his own predisposition he is going—unless he

55

reckons with the events which occurred in the Garden of Eden.

Therefore, we go back to the beginning chapters of the Bible, to the account of God making man in his image and placing him in the ideal environment of the Garden of Eden. *Eden* means "pleasure, delight." The Garden of Eden was God's delight; it was for man's pleasure. There has never been a spot on earth as "fair as Eden's Garden in all its beauty" (Joel 2:3). But it was this paradise that Satan invaded. That he was there is attested to in such passages as Ezekiel 28:13: "You were in Eden, the garden of God."

The biblical account (Genesis 2:7-22) of how God made the first man, Adam, and his wife, Eve, is a familiar one. He placed them in his indescribably beautiful paradise, where there were two conspicuous trees: the tree of life and the tree of the knowledge of good and evil. Enjoyment of the fruit of the former depended on abstinence from the fruit of the latter. Man, unlike the birds of the air, the animals of the field, and the fish of the sea, was made a free moral agent. He could chose to eat or not to eat of the fatal fruit. It was to be his own decision. Love is based on freedom. Adam and Eve lived in an absolutely ideal environment. In their hands was the destiny of the entire human race.

As we go to the account in Genesis 3, let us do so via Ezekiel, one of the major Israeli prophets from whom we drew most heavily for our biography of Satan. Ezekiel makes the point that Satan was almost irresistibly handsome as he came to Eve. As Shelley wrote in *Ozymandias*, "Sometimes the devil is a gentleman." "You [Satan] were in Eden, the garden of God; your clothing was bejeweled with every precious stone—ruby, topaz, diamond, chrysolite, onyx, jasper, sapphire, carbuncle, and

emerald—all in beautiful settings of finest gold"
(Ezekiel 23:13). It was enough to turn any woman's
head.

We tend to think that because Satan came to Eve
embodied as a serpent, he must have been repugnant,
as snakes are today. But Satan then, as a serpent, was
as attractive as a snake today is repulsive. You see, he
was walking upright. Only after God appeared in
judgment to Adam and Eve in the Garden of Eden did
he announce to the serpent: "You are singled out from
among all the domestic and wild animals of the
whole earth—to be cursed. You shall grovel in the
dust as long as you live, crawling along your belly"
(Genesis 3:14). The serpent was turned from the most
attractive creature on earth into one of the most feared
and repulsive.

But before his fall, "the serpent [the devil] was the
craftiest of all the creatures the Lord God had
made. So the serpent came to the woman. 'Really?'
he asked. 'None of the fruit in the garden? You mean
God says you mustn't eat *any* of it?'

" 'Of course we may eat it,' the woman told him.
'It's only the fruit from the tree at the *center* of the
garden that we are not to eat. God says we mustn't eat
it or even touch it, or we will die' " (Genesis 3:1-3).

The devil began his temptation of man with a dual ploy.
He questioned the word of God. This has been a
wedge-driving device of his ever since. Then he turned
Eve's attention to the one thing which God withheld:
the fruit of one tree. There were innumerable other
trees. There was delectable fruit and food in
abundance in every direction that Adam and Eve might
look. But Satan was a fifth columnist, a plant of his own
placing, a devil who had fallen himself.

Having set up Eve with a couple of preliminary
questions, he hisses at her, "That's a lie! You'll not

die! God knows very well that the instant you eat it you will become like him, for your eyes will be opened—you will be able to distinguish good from evil!'' (Genesis 3:4, 5). And his poisonous argument worked.

Did you know that there are several things the devil can do but Almighty God cannot do? For instance, the devil can tell a lie; God cannot lie. The devil can sin; God cannot sin. The devil can break his word; God cannot break his word. The devil can twist the truth; God cannot twist the truth. Here we have a prime example of the devil twisting the truth, and because man responded, Satan cut the jugular vein of the human race.

When Satan, with his hypnotic skill, suggested that Eve disobey God, she "was convinced. How lovely and fresh looking it was! and it would make her so wise! So she ate some of the fruit and gave some to her husband, and he ate it too. And as they ate it, suddenly they became aware of their nakedness and were embarrassed. So they strung fig leaves to cover themselves around the hips" (Genesis 3:6, 7).

The first man, Adam, had been swindled. Eve, the beautiful, virtuous first woman, had been carried away by Satan's intrigue, and her curiosity became a crushing monster. The serpent had coiled about her and strangled the human race.

From heading heavenward and eastward toward a perennially rising sun, man only freshly begun on this planet was already in eclipse and facing a dying day. His die had been cast—by Satan. The human race would be sired by an Adam whose legacy, whatever else he might transmit to his offspring, included sin deeply imbedded in the whole human race. Professor Suzuki, Canada's leading geneticist, recently declared at a medical convention that there is no scientific way whereby evil genes can be laundered out of the human bloodstream.

The rock group Blood, Sweat, and Tears have combined Mick Jagger's "Sympathy for the Devil" and Moussorgsky's "Night on Bald Mountain" in an album entitled "Sympathy for the Devil—Symphony to the Devil." Tragically and quickly Eve's "sympathy for the devil" had been turned into the human race rendering a "symphony to the devil," which is still playing and slaying today.

Man had sinned and was now Satan's pawn. As Feodor Dostoyevsky in *Brothers Karamazov* put it a century ago, "I think if the devil doesn't exist, but man has created him, he has created him in his own likeness." Man was in a terrible state indeed.

In the evening of that first sin-scarred day, Adam and Eve "heard the sound of the Lord God walking in the garden; and they hid themselves among the trees. The Lord God called to Adam, 'Why are you hiding?' " (Genesis 3:8, 9).

Why did God come on such a sin scene at all? Because when he made man, he made him for communion and companionship. Paul wrote to the delinquent Corinthians, "God is faithful, by whom ye were called unto the fellowship of his Son" (1 Corinthians 1:9, KJV). So when God called to Adam (he never coerces man or forces himself on man), "Adam replied, 'I heard you coming and didn't want you to see me naked. So I hid.'

" 'Who told you you were naked?' the Lord God asked. 'Have you eaten fruit from the tree I warned you about?'

" 'Yes,' Adam admitted, 'but it was the woman you gave me who brought me some, and I ate it' " (Genesis 3:10-12).

Adam tried to pass the buck. But there was no

passing of the buck of sin. The fact that Satan had intrigued Eve and that she had persuaded Adam was no excuse. Every man is responsible for his own sin and answerable for it.

Adam had sinned. Eve had sinned. The whole human race was doomed. "Yes, all have sinned; all fall short of God's glorious ideal" (Romans 3:23). It all began with the devil's visit to the Garden of Eden.

When Adam identified Eve as the human cause of sin, "The Lord God asked the woman, 'How could you do such a thing?' 'The serpent tricked me,' she replied" (Genesis 3:13).

It did not make Adam and Eve less guilty, but the human circulatory system *had* been tapped by the serpent's bite, and satanic venom had been injected into man's veins. It would be a poison never again absent from the human bloodstream.

Indeed, we read that several generations later "God saw that the wickedness of man was great in the earth, and that every imagination of the thoughts of his heart was only evil continually" (Genesis 6:5, KJV). As God looked at man, "he was sorry he had made them. It broke his heart" (Genesis 6:6).

When Adam and Eve sinned, the delight of God's heart had turned sour and he then had to pronounce judgment on man, woman, and serpent. So he "said to the serpent, 'This is your punishment: You are singled out from among all the domestic and wild animals of the whole earth—to be cursed. You shall grovel in the dust as long as you live, crawling along on your belly' " (Genesis 3:14). Then the Lord addressed Eve: "You shall bear children in intense pain and suffering; yet even so, you shall welcome your husband's affections, and he shall be your master" (Genesis 3:16).

Whatever social revolutions have occurred in history,

and despite agitations for change throughout the world today, woman and her role have never really changed since the Garden of Eden. She has wanted a husband. She has craved his leadership and his affection. She has undergone the pain of childbirth, to which she aspires and for which she eagerly suffers.

"And to Adam, God said, 'Because you listened to your wife and ate the fruit when I told you not to, I have placed a curse upon the soil. All your life you will struggle to extract a living from it. It will grow thorns and thistles for you, and you shall eat its grasses. All your life you will sweat to master it, until your dying day. Then you will return to the ground from which you came. For you were made from the ground, and to the ground you will return' " (Genesis 3:17-19).

Man's role has also not changed very much. He still is struggling desperately to extract from the soil sufficient food to feed the human race. He seems to be losing. As we fight the thorns and thistles, the weed controls and fertilizer we use contaminate our food supply. Our factories belch out pollutants over the earth. We seem to be moving closer to ecological disaster each day. It all began in the Garden of Eden. And from the Eden crisis to the current crises, man on this planet has sweated for a living, only to go back to the ground from which he came.

In paradise, lethal damage had been done. "So the Lord God banished him [man[forever from the Garden of Eden, and sent him out to farm the ground from which he had been taken. Thus God expelled him, and placed mighty angels at the east of the garden of Eden, with a flaming sword to guard the entrance to the Tree of Life" (Genesis 3:23, 24).

God had no other option than judgment for sin. "The wicked shall be sent away to hell," wrote King David;

"this is the fate of all the nations forgetting the Lord" (Psalm 9:17).

But wait a moment! Satan had successfully turned man away from God and started him on his way to hell. But now it was God's turn to intercept man with a redemptive plan. In Genesis 3:15 (the John 3:16 of the Old Testament), we read God's glorious promise: "And I will put the fear of you [the serpent] into the woman, and between your offspring and hers. He shall strike you on your head, while you will strike at his heel." That is the first prophecy of the coming of God the Son, Jesus Christ, as the Redeemer of anyone who would reject the devil and turn to Christ for salvation. Meanwhile, there was for Adam and Eve provision for their salvation. "The Lord God clothed Adam and his wife with garments made from skins of animals" (Genesis 3:21). It was the first occasion of bloodshed for sins. The blood of animals could not take away sin, but it would cover sin until the coming of the Redeemer. "Without the shedding of blood there is no forgiveness of sins" (Hebrews 9:22).

The first great rendezvous between Satan and man was the greatest disaster in human history. But because God is love, all was not lost.

The next recorded encounter between God, man, and Satan is recorded in Job. Though Job appears as the eighteenth book in the Old Testament, in terms of the events it records, it is second, Job living about the time of Abraham.

Job was a very wealthy man. "He owned 7,000 sheep, 3,000 camels, 500 teams of oxen, 500 female donkeys" (1:3). He had an enterprising family of seven sons and three daughters. But most of all, he was a devout and righteous man (1:1).

But "one day as the angels came to present themselves before the Lord, Satan, the Accuser, came with them" (1:6). From the dialogue and events which followed, we learn a great deal about Satan: his intent, his powers, and how he goes about his sinister work.

" 'Where have you come from?' the Lord asked Satan. And Satan replied, 'From patroling the earth.' Then the Lord asked Satan, 'Have you noticed my servant Job? He is the finest man in all the earth—a good man who fears God and will have nothing to do with evil.'

" 'Why shouldn't he, when you pay him so well?' Satan scoffed. 'You have always protected him and his home and his property from all harm. You have prospered everything he does—look how rich he is! No wonder he "worships" you! But just take away his wealth, and you'll see him curse you to your face!'

"And the Lord replied to Satan, 'You may do anything you like with his wealth, but don't harm him physically' " (1:7-13).

Here is one of the Scripture's most vivid descriptions of Satan at work. Satan talks with God about his people on earth and concentrates on how he can demean, deprecate, and condemn them. We discover he hates a man with integrity, especially a man who worships God. He'll fight such men any way he can.

He has enormous powers at his command. See what he did to Job:

"And the Lord replied to Satan, 'You may do anything you like with his wealth, but don't harm him physically.'

"So Satan went away; and sure enough, not long afterward when Job's sons and daughters were dining at the oldest brother's house, tragedy struck.

"A messenger rushed to Job's home with this news: 'Your oxen were plowing, with the donkeys feeding beside them, when the Sabeans raided us, drove away the animals and killed all the farmhands except me. I am the only one left.'

"While this messenger was still speaking, another arrived with more bad news: 'The fire of God has fallen down from heaven and burned up your sheep and all the herdsmen, and I alone have escaped to tell you.'

"Before this man finished, still another messenger rushed in: 'Three bands of Chaldeans have driven off your camels and killed your servants, and I alone have escaped to tell you.'

"As he was still speaking, another arrived to say, 'Your sons and daughters were feasting in their oldest brother's home, when suddenly a mighty wind swept in from the desert, and engulfed the house so that the roof fell in on them and all are dead; and I alone escaped to tell you' " (1:12-19).

What a merciless assault on one man! But note that God permitted Satan to unleash "tragedy" on Job, just as Jesus permitted the devil to sift Peter like wheat (Luke 22:31). It is a great assurance to know that Satan can never attack a believer without permission from the Lord.

The devil was allowed to incite the Sabeans and the Chaldeans to raid Job's property and to kill all his farmhands and employees—to a man. Satan was also allowed by God to send down such fire from the sky as to start a conflagration which devoured all Job's sheep and the herdsmen who attended them. Again, Satan was permited by God to so control the air currents that he caused a high wind to blast in from the desert and, during a birthday celebration being held by Job's ten children, collapse the roof of the house, killing them all.

Meanwhile, Job was in terrible distress. (He was not aware of the conversation in heaven.) But he did not renounce his trust in God though his grief was

almost unbearable. "Then Job stood up and tore his
robe in grief and fell down upon the ground before God.
'I came naked from my mother's womb,' he said, 'and
I shall have nothing when I die. The Lord gave me
everything I had, and they were his to take away.
Blessed be the name of the Lord.' In all of this, Job
did not sin or revile God" (1:20-22).

Satan might have left Job alone after that. But no, he
was determined to destroy Job. So "the angels came
again to present themselves before the Lord, and
Satan with them.

" 'Where have you come from?' the Lord asked
Satan.

" 'From patroling the earth,' Satan replied.

" 'Well, have you noticed my servant Job?' the Lord
asked. 'He is the finest man in all the earth—a good man
who fears God and turns away from all evil. And he
has kept his faith in me despite the fact that you
persuaded me to let you harm him without any cause.'

" 'Skin for skin,' Satan replied. 'A man will give
anything to save his life. Touch his body with sickness
and he will curse you to your face!'

" 'Do with him as you please,' the Lord replied; 'only
spare his life' " (2:1-6).

This would be most frightening to us if we did not
realize that God knew how strong Job's faith was. He
would not permit him to be tempted beyond his
spiritual capacity to resist, a principle Paul explained
to the Corinthians (1 Corinthians 10:13). God permits
only the strongest saints to be subjected to the strongest
tests. Out of the severest tests come the greatest
testimonies. Out of the deepest trials come the most
glorious triumphs. Job had what it took to be an
overcomer—indestructible faith in God.

Hence, God challenged Satan, " 'Do with him as
you please ... only spare his life.'

"So Satan went out from the presence of the Lord and struck Job with a terrible case of boils from head to foot. Then Job took a broken piece of pottery to scrape himself, and sat among the ashes.

"His wife said to him, 'Are you still trying to be godly when God has done all this to you? Curse him and die.'

"But he replied, 'You talk like some heathen woman. What? Shall we receive only pleasant things from the hand of God and never anything unpleasant?' So in all this Job said nothing wrong" (2:6-10).

Who won? What was the final score? God through his servant Job won; but not before Job lost his material wealth, his children, and the respect of his wife. He found only the relentless remonstrances of three of his friends and finally, the abject humiliation of an ash heap and the nearly intolerable pain of boils all over his body.

But Job stuck to his faith in God, and finally God drove off Satan and vindicated Job. He not only restored Job's previous wealth, but doubled it. He gave Job seven more sons and three beautiful daughters: Jemima, Kezia, and Keren. Moreover, God gave Job 140 years to enjoy "living a long, good life" (Job 42:12-17) as the head of his household of children, grandchildren, and great-grandchildren.

The third episode between God, the devil, and man recorded in the Old Testament involved Moses and the people of Israel. For over 400 years these people had lived in Egypt, seventy-one descendants of Jacob having multiplied into more than a million during that period of time. Meanwhile, the Pharaoh who had ruled Egypt when Joseph rescued the country was dead. The Pharaoh of Moses' day was a ruthless tyrant who oppressed the Hebrews without mercy.

God raised up Moses to deliver the Hebrew people.

Moses, called of God to go to Pharaoh, demanded on
God's behalf, "Let my people go!" They wished to
go out across the Red Sea through the wilderness to
Israel (Exodus 5:1-3), the land God had promised them.
The request did not please Pharaoh.

In a later confrontation, Moses' brother Aaron
threw down his rod and the rod became a serpent. But
to Moses' amazement, the magicians of Egypt were
also able to perform this feat. Undoubtedly Satan
was present to turn their rods into serpents. The
serpent of Moses and Aaron devoured the magicians'
serpents, but this miracle was not sufficient to convince
Pharaoh to let Israel go (7:8-14).

The next day Moses and Aaron again went before
Pharaoh, and this time Aaron turned Moses' rod
toward the Nile. The great river turned into blood,
as did all the waters in the land, even the water stored
in bowls and pots in the homes of the people. What a
miracle of judgment! But Pharaoh's devil-empowered
agents "used their secret arts and they, too, turned
water into blood" (7:15-22). So the contest was still on.
Pharaoh would not give in.

The following week, Moses and Aaron again
went in before Pharaoh, and when he again refused
their request, they invoked Jehovah's power to bring
frogs up out of the Nile to swarm through the homes of
Egypt. How could the Egyptians live with frogs
jumping into their ovens, their kneading bowls, and
even into their beds? But the devil was not to be
beaten. For "the magicians did the same with their
secret arts, and they, too, caused frogs to come upon
the land" (8:1-7). Perhaps the Lord was permitting
Moses, like Job, to be tested by the devil.

Things were different with the third plague. We read
that "the Lord said to Moses, 'Tell Aaron to strike the
dust with his rod, and it will become lice, throughout

all the land of Egypt.' So Moses and Aaron did as God commanded, and suddenly lice infested the entire nation, covering the Egyptians and their animals. Then the magicians tried to do the same thing with their secret arts, but this time they failed. 'This is the finger of God,' they exclaimed to Pharaoh'' (8:16-19). Satan had obviously now extended himself to his outer limits, and God stepped in to vindicate his servant Moses and his people Israel.

Pharaoh and the Egyptians did not let Israel go easily. God sent seven more plagues to ravage the land and the people before Pharaoh agreed to free the Hebrews (8:20—13:18). But the decisive point in the contest was when the agents of the devil were obliged to concede, "This is the finger of God."

Israel was safely out of Egypt and well into the wilderness when the Lord gave them the ten major commandments, along with a complete set of laws to implement these commandments. The people were amply warned to avoid any kind of dealing with the devil.

God's first commandment was directed against the devil himself: "You may worship no other god than me" (20:3). What other god could there be? Satan. The second commandment was, "You shall not make yourselves any idols [or] any images" (20:4). From the pronouncements of David in the Old Testament and Paul in the New, as we'll see later, worshiping idols is demon worship.

God strictly forbade his people to sacrifice to "evil spirits [demons] out in the fields" (Leviticus 17:7). He also commanded, "Do not defile yourselves by consulting mediums and wizards, for I am Jehovah your God" (19:31). Indeed, he said through Moses, "I will set my face against anyone who consults mediums and wizards instead of me and I will cut that

person off from his people" (20:6). The practice was not
only so serious as to warrant excommunication, but "a
medium or a wizard—whether man or woman—shall
surely be stoned to death. They have caused their own
doom" (20:27). It would seem that Jehovah meant
that these people were beyond the point of
redemption. "The people of Israel also killed Balaam
the magician, the son of Beor" (Joshua 13:22).

As Moses approached the end of his earthly
journey, he concentrated on Israel's conduct. In his
concluding addresses to them, he ordered, "When you
arrive in the Promised Land you must be very
careful." They were to be constantly vigilant, for
"no Israeli may practice black magic, or call on the evil
spirits for aid, or to be a fortune teller, or a serpent
charmer, medium, or wizard, or call forth the spirits of
the dead. Anyone doing these things is an object of
horror and disgust to the Lord." They were warned
that "the Lord your God will not permit you to do
such things" (Deuteronomy 18:9-14).

Throughout ancient Hebrew history, there was a
seesaw battle in the hearts of the people between serving
the true God and the gods which were put forth by the
devil.

When Israel wanted a king despite God's will to the
contrary, God permitted them to choose Saul. He
was a real paradox, because during his reign he had
the courage of his convictions and "banned all mediums
and wizards from the land of Israel" (1 Samuel 28:3). But
later he turned around and sought out the services of a
medium. The following day he committed suicide after
being vanquished by the Philistines (28:7, 8; 31:3, 4).

Saul was succeeded by David. So important a
man was David in the kingdom of Israel and in the
plans of God (he was "a man after God's own heart"),
that the devil seems to have paid him a personal visit, as

we saw earlier. "Satan stood up against Israel, and provoked David..." (1 Chronicles 21:1, KJV) and David capitulated to his pressure. Seventy thousand men died because of God's judgment (21:14).

King David's son Solomon kept the kingdom intact, but his successors, Kings Jeroboam and Rehoboam, split it into the kingdoms of Israel and Judah. Jeroboam was a disaster for Israel, for he turned his back on the true God and "appointed other priests instead who encouraged the people to worship idols instead of God, and to sacrifice to carved statues of goats and calves which he placed on the hills" (2 Chronicles 11:14, 15).

The situation in the kingdom of Israel deteriorated rapidly. Ahab married Jezebel, an idol-worshiper. With Ahab's death, the devil came even more out into the open under the name of Baal-zebub. "Israel's new king, Ahaziah, had fallen off the upstairs porch of his palace at Samaria and was seriously injured. He sent messengers to the temple of the god Baal-zebub at Ekron to ask whether he would recover. But an angel of the Lord told Elijah the prophet, 'Go and meet the messengers and ask them, "Is it true that there is no God in Israel? Is that why you are going to Baal-zebub?" ... 'Because you [King Ahaziah] have done this, you shall not leave this bed; you will surely die.' " And die he did (2 Kings 1:1-17).

Few writers in the history of literature have written with such poignance and power as the prophet Isaiah. He lived in Judah, the southern kingdom, which had not apostasized as quickly as Israel (the northern kingdom). But by the time he came on the scene, the situation was deteriorating. He witnessed the reign and death of good King Hezekiah, and then the tragedy of one of the worst kings who ever lived, King Manasseh. God through Isaiah said to Judah in those

days, "You witches' sons, you offspring of adulterers
and harlots!... You worship your idols with great zeal
beneath the shade of every tree, and slay your
children as human sacrifices down in the valleys,
under overhanging rocks.... Behind closed doors you
set your idols up and worship someone other than me."
Who was this someone? Obviously the devil, who was
behind the god Molech. Isaiah pronounced, "This is
adultery, for you are giving these idols your love,
instead of loving me." There it is—idolatry (demon
worship) is spiritual adultery. And Isaiah points out
the length to which these people went: "You have
traveled far, even to hell itself, to find new gods to love.
You grew weary in your search, but you never gave
up" (Isaiah 57:3-10).

King Manasseh, it might be said, established demon
worship as the religion of his kingdom. We read that
"heathen altars to the sun god, moon god, and the
gods of the stars were placed even in the Temple of the
Lord—in the very city and building which the Lord had
selected to honor his own name. And he sacrificed one
of his sons as a burnt offering on a heathen altar. He
practiced black magic and used fortune-telling, and
patronized mediums and wizards. So the Lord was
very angry ... Manasseh enticed them to do even
more evil than the surrounding nations had done, even
though Jehovah destroyed those nations for their evil
ways" (2 Kings 21:3-9).

Yet this evil man was the prodigal son of the Old
Testament. He went into the Babylonian captivity,
and there he repented. God brought him back to
Jerusalem and gave Judah one more chance
(2 Chronicles 33:11-19).

During part of the period just before the great
seventy-year captivity of all Israel in Babylon, Josiah,
the best king since King David, occupied the throne. He

THE DEVIL

was great because he prepared to purge the land of
demon worship and turn, with his people, to the
true God. We read that King Josiah "exterminated
the mediums and wizards, and every kind of idol
worship, both in Jerusalem and throughout the land. For
Josiah wanted to follow all the laws which were
written in the book that Hilkiah the priest had found in
the Temple. There was no other king who so
completely turned to the Lord and followed all the
laws of Moses" (2 Kings 23:24, 25).

But King Josiah was the last to stand up to the devil
and replace demon worship with the worship of the true
God. The Israelites were carried off to Babylon, and
Gentiles occupied their mother city Jerusalem until
A.D. 1967.

The devil knew that the prophets had predicted
that the Messiah was to be born in Bethlehem of a
Hebrew virgin. He was understandably determined that
under no circumstances would he let the Jews be restored
to their homeland—not if he could help it.

But God was seeing to it that Israel would return; and
spearheading the vanguard were Ezra, Nehemiah, and
Zerubbabel. Satan tried to intervene. The prophet
Zechariah recorded what happened. "Then the
Angel showed me (in my vision) Joshua the High Priest
standing before the Angel of the Lord; and Satan was
there too, at the Angel's right hand, accusing Joshua of
many things. And the Lord said to Satan, 'I reject your
accusations, Satan; yes, I, the Lord, for I have
decided to be merciful to Jerusalem—I rebuke you.
I have decreed mercy to Joshua and his nation; they
are like a burning stick pulled out of the fire' "
(Zechariah 3:1, 2).

And by that act, God Almighty preserved the way
for the coming of the Redeemer, who would vanquish
Satan and his kingdom of demons.

CHAPTER FIVE

Why Jesus Came

Why did Christ become a man?

The Apostle John made it clear: "For this purpose the Son of God was manifested, that he might destroy the works of the devil" (1 John 3:8, KJV). Why did the New Testament authors pass their message on to us? John explained that he had "written, that ye might believe that Jesus is the Christ, the Son of God; and that believing ye might have life through his name" (John 20:31, KJV). The New Testament is essentially the account of Jesus, the Son of God, subduing Satan, the betrayer of man.

Because God the Son came to vanquish the devil, Satan often attempts to deflect people from Christ by denying that he came as a man. John predicted that just before Jesus' return, the "spirit of antichrist" would be abroad and believers would need to be especially careful. So he gave us this test: "Every spirit that confesseth that Jesus Christ is come in the flesh is of God: And every spirit [demon] that confesseth not that Jesus Christ is come in the flesh is not of God" (1 John 4:2, 3, KJV).

The devil, of course, knows that Jesus Christ as God the Son did indeed come in the flesh, but he is doing everything in his power to keep people throughout the world oblivious of or antagonistic to this fact.

As we go back to the time when Jesus was born, we discover that Satan and his kingdom of demons were mobilized and ready. He very much wanted to destroy the Child Jesus. So he worked through Herod, the king of Judea, who was told that the future King of the Jews would be born in Bethlehem. Herod, unable to lay his hands on the Child by manipulating the wise men from the East, killed every baby boy, two years old and under, in the entire region of Bethlehem. God, knowing all things, told Joseph to take Mary and the Child into Egypt. When they returned to Israel after the death of Herod, they settled in Nazareth, in Galilee. There Jesus grew to manhood. The devil had lost.

The longer Jesus remained invulnerable to Satan's temptation attacks, the more firepower the devil put into them. But Jesus stood like the Rock of Gibraltar through the severest of storms. No man had ever done so before. The devil was baffled and angry, but Jesus never flinched. He came through unscathed. He could not have done otherwise, for he was God.

The writer of Hebrews gives us a glimpse of how relentlessly Satan attacked Jesus' character during his earthly life. "Since we, God's children, are human beings—made of flesh and blood—he became flesh and blood too by being born into human form; for only as a human being could he die and in dying break the

power of the devil who had the power of death'' (2:14).
If Jesus had come down and lived only a week or two,
or given only those three years of public ministry
before dying on the cross, he would have been a
plastic messiah, not the real Christ. The writer to the
Hebrews goes on: "He did not come as an angel but as a
human being ... And it was necessary for Jesus to be like
us, brothers, so that he could be our merciful and
faithful High Priest before God, a Priest who would be
both merciful to us and faithful to God in dealing with
the sins of the people. For since he himself has now
been through suffering and temptation, he knows
what it is like when we suffer and are tempted, and he is
wonderfully able to help us" (2:16-18).

It is important to note this carefully, for two
reasons. One, it shows us that Jesus never once sinned.
He "knew no sin," Paul declared (2 Corinthians 5:21,
KJV); he "did no sin," Peter pointed out (1 Peter
2:22, KJV); and John assured us that "in him is no
sin" (1 John 3:5, KJV). Yet he knew the pressure of
temptation from Satan, temptation pressure which
probably increased as Jesus approached his public
ministry.

Why did the pressure increase? Here is our second
reason for noting the significance of Jesus' temptation:
he was the only man who successfully resisted every
assault of Satan and his demons. This is what finally
convinced Satan that here was the unique Man.
From the time he had heard the announcement in the
Garden of Eden, he had always known that the Christ
was coming. But he did not know when. Then one night,
an angel announced to some shepherds that the
Messiah had been born. Thirty years later he was to
receive a personal visit from Satan, who tried to make
him slip—just once!

Matthew, Mark, and Luke write about Jesus' forty

days in a barren and lonely wilderness, where he faced the king of demons himself. The precipitating factor was Jesus' baptism. Our Lord went all the way from Nazareth in Galilee to the place where John the Baptist was baptizing people in the Jordan River. There he went down into the water and was baptized. "The moment Jesus came up out of the water, he saw the heavens open and the Holy Spirit in the form of a dove descending on him, and a voice from heaven said, 'You are my beloved Son; you are my Delight.' Immediately the Holy Spirit urged Jesus into the desert" (Mark 1:10-12).

Why did the Holy Spirit urge Jesus into the wilderness? Because "there, for forty days, alone except for desert animals, he was subjected to Satan's temptations to sin" (Mark 1:12, 13). One might ask: Was he really tempted as we are tempted? Yes! And indescribably worse. The devil came at Jesus with a hurricane of temptation. We often say, "My temptation is not your temptation, and your temptation is not my temptation." Jesus suffered every temptation known to man in life, as in death he was to suffer every pain known to man. The writer to the Hebrews said, "He had the same temptations we do, though he never once gave way to them and sinned" (Hebrews 4:15).

At the baptism scene, a vigilant Satan had heard the very voice of God signal from heaven that Jesus was indeed his Son. He rushed to the scene; he must be on the spot for a one-to-one encounter. After fasting for forty days and forty nights, Jesus was "very hungry" (Luke 4:2). Consequently, Satan pounced on the idea of exploiting to the hilt the physical appetite of our Lord. "Satan said, 'If you are God's Son, tell this stone to become a loaf of bread' " (Luke 4:3). That sounded logical enough. But Jesus, being the Son of God, was not on earth to obey Satan's challenges or follow his suggestions. He had come to destroy the works of the devil (1 John 3:8); he could never destroy Satan by obeying him. Moreover, Jesus had not come to minister to himself, but to others (Mark 10:45). Nor had he come to prove to Satan that he was the Son of God. Satan was already well aware of who he was.

Jesus answers Satan's challenge by quoting from the Word of God: "It is written in the Scriptures, 'Other things in life are much more important than bread' " (Luke 4:4). Jesus was not saying that eating bread was wrong. He wasn't even saying that it was wrong to turn a stone into a loaf of bread and eat it. He was demonstrating the fact that he had an immeasurably higher authority than Satan, and in no way would he obey the instructions or the suggestions of the devil. If the devil tells us to do something which doesn't seem wrong, it is wrong simply because the devil told us to do it. In other words, Jesus told the devil, "The Scriptures tell us that bread won't feed men's souls: obedience to every word of God is what we need" (Matthew 4:4).

Then "Satan took him to Jerusalem to the roof of the Temple. 'Jump off,' he said, 'and prove you are the Son of God; for the Scriptures declare, "God will send his angels to keep you from harm," ... they will prevent you from smashing on the rocks below.' Jesus retorted, 'It also says not to put the Lord your God to a foolish test' " (Matthew 4:5-7).

The devil was apparently embodied in as human a form as was Jesus. In the wilderness he could have appeared in any number of forms. But to be able to walk with Jesus through the maze of people in Jerusalem and ascend to the roof of the Temple without attracting undue attention would seem to indicate that Satan, as an angel, elected to appear on this

77

occasion in a body. This is biblically feasible, for angels, Paul taught, do have bodies (1 Corinthians 15:40). That an evil spirit could and did appear from time to time in a form that looked as physical as a man is indicated in such passages as Matthew 14:26. Jesus suddenly and unexpectedly appeared to his disciples, and they shouted, " 'It is a spirit'; and they cried out for fear" (KJV).

Why did Jesus not jump from the Temple as Satan suggested? Because he was not on earth as a trapeze artist, nor was he on an ego trip. His was an errand of grace. He was not on tour as an exhibitionist, but on a Shepherd's quest for lost sheep. No one, least of all the devil, is "to put the Lord your God to a foolish test." Jesus never once invoked the angels to come and rescue him from a contrived emergency. He could have. He later told his captors that were he to so order, he could beckon thousands of angels to come and protect him (Matthew 26:53). But he had not come to avoid ordeal. He had come to serve, to suffer, to bleed, to die, to save. Jesus was saying, in effect, that he had come to be involved, not to escape.

Finally, "Satan took him to the peak of a very high mountain and showed him the nations of the world and all their glory. 'I'll give it all to you,' he said, 'if you will only kneel and worship me' " (Matthew 4:8, 9).

Here Satan laid claim to the domination and glory of the nations of the world, and Jesus did not argue with him. But Jesus would have none of Satan's bribery. His would be the repossession of all the world and the glory thereof, but it would not happen if he fell down and worshiped Satan. Rather, it would happen when he would give up his life on the cross. He was not going into a bargain basement with the devil to make a cheap deal. He would not sell out under any circumstances. He was too true to his Father for that; he loved men too much. His integrity and his eternity eliminated this option. And this time he spoke sharply to the devil: "Get out of here, Satan... The Scriptures say, 'Worship only the Lord God. Obey only him' " (Matthew 4:10).

Satan, knowing that Christ said what he meant and meant what he said, "left Jesus for a while and went away" (Luke 4:13). He had no other choice. In three ways he had been thwarted by our Lord: Jesus was filled with the Holy Spirit; he was devoted to doing the will of his Father; he quoted Scripture.

Jesus had declared war on Satan and his whole kingdom of demons. After all, he had come to "destroy the works of the devil" (1 John 3:8, KJV), and from Jesus' temptation to the cross, it was an all-out, hammer-and-tongs, knock-down-drag-out battle. Satan mobilized the forces at his command, holding back no reserves. But Jesus would not give in. Every word he spoke, every deed he did, every offensive he launched was a frontal attack in his strategy to "destroy the works of the devil."

It is noteworthy that Jesus flatly refused to demonstrate to Satan that he was indeed the Son of God by turning a stone into a loaf of bread. But when some were in honest search, he did not hesitate to let them know that he was indeed the Christ, the Son of God. For example, John the Baptist had seemed to be sure that Jesus was the Messiah. But when he was arrested and imprisoned by Herod, he succumbed to despondency and began to wonder. So "he sent two of his disciples to Jesus to ask him, 'Are you really the Messiah? Or shall we keep on looking for him?' The two disciples found Jesus ... casting out evil spirits [demons]." When they confronted him with John's question, this was his reply: "Go back to John and tell him all you have seen and heard here today" (Luke 7:19-22).

The Pharisees once accused Jesus of being Satan. (Keep in mind that the Pharisees, unlike the Sadducees, definitely believed in the spirit world, as seen in Acts 23:8, 9.) Jesus replied, "If I am casting out demons by the Spirit of God, then the Kingdom of God has arrived among you. One cannot rob Satan's kingdom without first binding Satan. Only then can his demons be cast out! Anyone who isn't helping me is harming me" (Matthew 12:28-30). The devil was aggressive and needed to be aggressively attacked and defeated, said Jesus. "For when Satan, strong and fully armed, guards his palace, it is safe—until someone stronger and better-armed attacks and overcomes him and strips him of his weapons and carries off his belongings" (Luke 11:21, 22). With the arrival of Jesus on the scene, Satan confronted someone much "stronger and better-armed." Jesus went on the offensive soon after his triumph over Satan in the desert.

In Capernaum Jesus had his first recorded exchange with demons. He entered the synagogue and "a man possessed by a demon was present and began shouting, 'Why are you bothering us, Jesus of Nazareth—have you come to destroy us demons? I know who you are—the holy Son of God!' Jesus curtly commanded the demon to say no more and to come out of the man. At that the evil spirit screamed and convulsed the man violently and left him. Amazement gripped the audience and they began discussing what had happened. 'What sort of new religion is this?' they asked excitedly. 'Why, even evil spirits obey his orders!' " (Mark 1:23-27).

This was no matter of playing mere games. It was a duel in which Jesus established his authority over demons. That day "by sunset the courtyard [of Peter's house] was filled with the sick and demon-possessed," wrote Mark. Not only did Jesus order the "demons to come out of their victims," but "he refused to allow the demons to speak" (Mark 1:32-34). He had not come to dialogue with the devil or his demons, but to defeat and destroy them.

Thus Jesus set out to challenge the occupation of human life by Satan and his demons. He demonstrated such authority over the devil and his army that they released their victims at his word. Matthew wrote, "That evening several demon-possessed people were brought to Jesus; and when he spoke a single word, all the demons fled" (8:16). Indeed, they would readily acknowledge him to be the Son of God, even though they might cry out with rage and dismay. Mark noted that "unclean spirits [not only the victims], when they saw him, fell down before him, and cried, saying, 'Thou art the Son of God' " (3:11, KJV).

And well they might, for they had intimidated and victimized those whom they possessed with ruthlessness and nearly unbelievable cruelty. There was, for instance, a woman mentioned only by Luke whose story speaks for itself. "There was a woman which had a spirit of infirmity" (13:11, KJV). She was so "seriously handicapped" that she had "been bent double for eighteen years and was unable to straighten herself" (TLB). Jesus plainly attributed this to "bondage in which Satan has held her for eighteen years" (13:16).

So Jesus said, with his unique kind of love, " 'Woman, you are healed of your sickness.' He touched her, and instantly she could stand straight. How she praised and thanked God!" (13:12, 13). Wouldn't anyone of us have done so, if we had been in this helpless woman's state? This does not mean, of course, that all sick people are possessed of demons. But some who display the kind of symptoms this woman had may be.

The devil would rob other people of their speech. Luke recorded the incident in which "once, when Jesus cast out a demon from a man who couldn't speak, his voice returned to him. The crowd was excited and enthusiastic" (11:14). Who wouldn't be, anyone who had a heart at all? Here was a man who had been dumb; now he could speak.

But some wouldn't be able to hear him. There was a man who was deaf, and also afflicted with a speech problem. Mark wrote, "A deaf man with a speech impediment was brought to him, and everyone begged Jesus to lay his hands on the man and heal him" (7:32).

A part of Jesus' demonstration of his deity was his variety of therapeutic methods; his techniques could not be codified. In this instance, "Jesus led him away from the crowd and put his fingers into the man's ears, then spat and touched the man's tongue with the spittle. Then, looking up to heaven, he sighed and commanded, 'Open!' Instantly the man could hear perfectly and speak plainly" (7:33-35). Is it any wonder that the crowd who pressed behind Jesus and had by now caught up "were overcome with utter amazement. Again and again they said, 'Everything he does is wonderful!' " (7:37).

Then there was the boy who was brought to Jesus who, among other things, was also completely deaf. " 'O demon of deafness and dumbness,' he said, 'I command you to come out of this child and enter him no more!' " (Mark 9:25). The demon left—unwillingly. "The demon screamed terribly and convulsed the boy again and left him; and the boy lay there limp and motionless, to all appearance dead. A murmur ran

through the crowd—'he is dead.' But Jesus took him
by the hand and helped him to his feet and he stood up
and was all right!'' (9:26, 27).

Mark also writes about a despised Gentile woman
"whose little girl was possessed by a demon" (7:25).
Here was a family in distress. They had perhaps tried
every conceivable means of therapy, but none
worked. Then this Syrophoenician mother heard that
Jesus was in the area, and she went to him. When she
arrived she "fell at his feet, and pled with him to release
her child from the demon's control" (7:25, 26). Only a
parent who has had a child in a really distressing state
could empathize with a woman who ignored racial and
social barriers to get help for her daughter. Jesus,
who tempted no one, tested this woman's faith by
indicating that he should first minister to the Jewish
people. But she was not prepared to take no for an
answer. She begged him to extend his mercy to the
despised.

But the disciples were not willing to be so generous.
Matthew writes that they "urged [Jesus] to send her
away. 'Tell her to get going,' they said, 'for she is
bothering us with all her begging' " (15:23).

But the woman—what a mother she was—"worshiped
him and pled again, 'Sir, help me!' " (15:25). And
Jesus, who has never sent away a needy person who
asks for help, declared, "Woman, your faith is large,
and your request is granted" (15:28). "I have
healed your little girl. Go on home, for the demon has
left her!" (Mark 7:29). The woman had a long trek
home, but her elation and gratitude to Jesus must have
known no bounds, for "when she arrived home, her
little girl was lying quietly in bed, and the demon was
gone" (7:30).

How many people from whom Jesus exorcised
demons we do not know. John concluded his Gospel

with the statement that he would "suppose that if all the other events in Jesus' life were written, the whole world could hardly contain the books" (John 21:25).

But Jesus had not come just to demonstrate that he was the Son of God by doing humanitarian services for his earthly contemporaries. He had come to "destroy the works of the devil"—if not immediately, ultimately! And this he could only do by dying. He said, "I, the Messiah, am not here to be served, but to help others, and to give my life as a ransom for many" (Mark 10:45).

The devil feared Jesus, for he would be the death knell spelling defeat for Satan and his demon kingdom—forever. Even when Jesus cast out many demons, as he did from the maniac of Gadara, he had his crucifixion on his mind, by which he would break the back of Satan's kingdom on earth. Jesus announced, "I, the Messiah, shall also suffer." And, "I am going to be betrayed into the power of those who will kill me, and on the third day afterwards I will be brought back to life again" (Matthew 17:12, 23). To cast out demons was to treat a wound. But by dying, Jesus would root out the evil cause of all the world's ills and provide a redemptive cure for all believers.

Joseph Parker, a great London preacher of a century ago, once said that Jesus was never off his cross until he was nailed to it, for he was "the Lamb slain from the foundation of the world" (Revelation 13:8, KJV). Before Jesus came to this earth, and throughout his earthly life, he was committed to his redemptive atonement on the cross.

We see this in the "Good Shepherd" chapter, John 10. Jesus had referred to the devil as a thief (v. 10) and as a wolf (v. 12). To save his people from the thief of their souls and from their attacker, Jesus promised to give his life: "I lay down my life voluntarily. For I have the right and power to lay it down when I want to and also the right and power to take it again. For the Father has given me this right" (v. 18). The wonderful thing is that he *wants* to give his life. The ironic thing is that when his critics heard him say this, they completely misunderstood him. "When he said these things, the Jewish leaders were again divided in their opinions about him. Some of them said, 'He has a demon or else is crazy. Why listen to a man like that?' Others said, 'This doesn't sound to us like a man possessed by a demon! Can a demon open the eyes of blind men?' " (vv. 19-21).

As Jesus approached the cross, sometimes the burden of it got to him. " 'Shall I pray, "Father, save me from what lies ahead"? But that is the very reason why I came! Father, bring glory and honor to your name.' Then a voice spoke from heaven saying, 'I have already done this, and I will do it again.' " The crowd around him heard the sound of the voice. "Jesus told them, 'The voice was for your benefit, not mine. The time of judgment for the world has come—and the time when Satan, the prince of this world, shall be cast out. And when I am lifted up [on the cross], I will draw everyone to me.' He said this to indicate how he was going to die" (John 12:27-33).

Finally our Lord's time came when "through death he [would] destroy him that had the power of death, that is, the devil" (Hebrews 2:14, KJV). And here was one of the most amazing ironies of history. The devil was anxious to ensure our Lord's death from the time Jesus was born into the world; yet it was by Jesus' death, which the devil did everything in his power to arrange, that he was defeated.

"Jesus knew on the evening of Passover Day that it would be his last night on earth before returning to his Father. During supper the devil had already suggested to Judas Iscariot, Simon's son, that this was the night to carry out his plan to betray Jesus" (John 13:1, 2). The crucifixion took place, and with the Son of God hanging on the center cross, the devil thought he had won. But he read the scoreboard upside down. He had actually lost, and it was just a matter of time until his doom would be sealed forever.

As Jesus hung on the cross, he signed in blood his will for a world lost in helpless spiritual poverty and in hopeless alienation from Father God. He was determined to provide the total price to redeem human souls from the bondage of the devil and to meet their entire earthly and eternal needs. So, desolate and alone on the cross, he cried, "My God, my God, why hast thou forsaken me?" (Matthew 27:46, KJV). His Father had to turn his back upon him, because he was made "sin for us, who knew no sin; that we might be made the righteousness of God in him" (2 Corinthians 5:21, KJV). Well did Jesus know that the Roman soldiers were pawns in the devil's hands that day. He cried out, "Father, forgive them; for they know not what they do" (Luke 23:34, KJV).

As Jesus continued to hang in terrible agony of spirit and body, he cried, "I'm thirsty" (John 19:28). Mocking, maligning soldiers offered him "sour wine" (Luke 23:36) to sedate him. But he refused. He was carrying the guilt of all people throughout all ages in a vicarious, atoning death. The devil could not succeed in diverting him from the redemption of repentant men.

Yet while carrying the guilt and burdens of men through the ages, he was sensitive to the needs of the people gathered on Calvary. He said to his mother Mary, " 'Woman, behold thy Son.' Then saith he to the disciple [John], 'Behold thy mother' " (John 19:26, 27, KJV). He cared for the most virtuous in society; he also cared for the least. To the repentant criminal hanging on a nearby cross Jesus said, "To-day shalt thou be with me in paradise" (Luke 23:43, KJV). That was surely snatching a soul as a brand from the burning! Just as that condemned wretch was being pushed through the gates of hell, Jesus, the Son of God, rescued him from the hold of Satan.

When Jesus cried, "It is finished" (John 19:30, KJV), the price of man's ransom had been paid—in full. Jesus then committed himself to his Father: "Father, into thy hands I commend my spirit" (Luke 23:46, KJV).

The Son of God upset Satan's plot and "having spoiled principalities and powers, he made a show of them openly, triumphing over them in it" (Colossians 2:15, KJV). At the moment of Jesus' death, "the earth shook, and the rocks broke, and tombs opened... The soldiers at the crucifixion and their sergeant were terribly frightened by the earthquake and all that happened. They exclaimed, 'Surely this was God's Son!' " (Matthew 27:51-54).

It is significant that "early on Sunday morning when Jesus came back to life ... the first person who saw him was Mary Magdalene—the woman from whom he had cast out seven demons" (Mark 16:9). Could the devil have tried to "recapture" her, and did she need special reassurance from her Savior?

During the forty days after his resurrection, Jesus gave to the disciples his final instructions: "You are to go into all the world and preach the Good News to everyone, everywhere... Those who believe shall use my authority to cast out demons" (Mark 16:15, 17). This was to be a part of the power they would receive on the day of Pentecost after a ten-day period of waiting on God in prayer (Acts 1:8—2:4).

THE DEVIL

As the apostles went everywhere to everyone they could contact, they walked in the resurrection power of Jesus—the power of the Holy Spirit over the devil and his demons. Crowds came to them including those "possessed by demons; and every one of them was healed" (Acts 5:16). As it was in Jerusalem, so it was in Samaria where "the evil spirits were cast out, screaming as they left their victims ... there was much joy in that city" (Acts 8:7). These events were to be only the beginning of a ministry to the whole world.

Perhaps the most succinct statement of our Lord's "new testament in my blood" (1 Corinthians 11:25, KJV) as a weapon against the attacks of the devil was made by Paul when he explained to Agrippa what the Good News was all about. Jesus told Paul he sent his followers to people in the world "to open their eyes to their true condition so that they may repent and live in the light of God instead of in Satan's darkness, so that they may receive forgiveness for their sins and God's inheritance along with all people everywhere whose sins are cleansed away, who are set apart by faith in me" (Acts 26:18).

Jesus' final conquest of Satan is depicted vividly in The Revelation. Christ will come again from heaven to defeat the devil with his assembled armies at Armageddon. And for 1,000 years Satan will be subdued. Armageddon, however, will be the putting down, but not the final putting out of Satan. Satan will be bound for the millennium of Christ's kingdom on earth. Lion and lamb will lie down together, with swords being beaten into plowshares and spears into pruning hooks.

But Satan will have one more short spree before being taken into the custody of eternal hell. At the end of the 1,000 years of peace and prosperity on this earth, "Satan will be let out of his prison. He will go out to

deceive the nations of the world and gather them
together, with Gog and Magog, for battle—a mighty
host, numberless as sand along the shore. They will
go up across the broad plain of the earth and
surround God's people and the beloved city of
Jerusalem on every side. But fire from God in heaven will
flash down on the attacking armies and consume them.
Then the devil who had betrayed them will again be
thrown into the Lake of Fire ... and they will be
tormented day and night forever and ever"
(Revelation 20:7-10).

At last right will have prevailed. Wrong will have
been put down forever. Jesus Christ's eternal triumph
will be in effect.

CHAPTER SIX

The Devil on Main Street

The devil seems to run his kingdom on this earth chiefly as an undercover agency. His is a submarine fleet. It is not to his advantage to show himself normally, because that would confirm his existence and could cause us to concentrate on devising effective defenses.

Cooperation from people is best achieved by the devil's communicating with them through spirit beings. By using the spirit vehicle, Satan is capable of an almost infinite variety of attacks.

It is important to keep this in mind as we look at Satan's manifestations. We would not expect Satan or the demons at his command to appear bodily to men, except when it is in the devil's interest for them to do so.

In almost any airport, Main Street, suburban plaza, and university bookstore you will find racks or stacks of books dealing with themes of the occult, devil worship, divination, and astrology. In Foyles, London's world-famous bookstore, there is a whole wall full of books on these themes. In addition, profits are pouring in for the manufacturers of ritual robes, crystal balls, Ouija boards, tarot cards, rabbits' feet, amulets, special herb incense. Satan-style clothes, such as those complete with horn and cloven hoof designs, red tunics, bushy tails, and goat-like headdresses.

How do demons assert their power while remaining as anonymous as possible? Every man has in him what Tolstoy described as a "God-shaped blank." Without God, a man is wide open to demon possession. In fact, Jesus said that it is tragic enough for a man to have one demon in him. But if that demon induces "seven other demons" to join him and "all enter the man ... the poor fellow is seven times worse off than he was before" (Luke 11:24-26). A case of someone who had seven demons in her was Mary Magdalene. After Jesus exorcised these demons, she became one of his most faithful followers. With his twelve disciples and some devout women, she went on Jesus' great "tour of the cities and villages of Galilee to announce the coming of the Kingdom of God." Others of the women "from whom he had cast out demons" (Luke 8:1, 2) also went along with Jesus, but the fact that Luke points out Mary Magdalene seems to indicate that seven demons were a heavy load and a major tragedy.

Is it any wonder that the maniac of Gadara was a wild man, "filled with" many demons as he was (Luke 8:30)? Is it any wonder that no one could subdue him? He broke apart even the strongest of chains as if he were snapping threads. He ran about naked. He shrieked like a siren. He cut himself up. He lived in a cemetery. He "had been demon-possessed for a long time'' (8:27), perhaps most of his life. Then Jesus came.

One day a father approached Jesus with his son. He lamented, "Teacher, this boy here is my only son, and a demon keeps seizing him, making him scream; and it throws him into convulsions so that he foams at the mouth; it is always hitting him and hardly ever leaves him alone" (Luke 9:38, 39). Moreover, Matthew notes, the father said he was "mentally deranged ... he often falls into the fire or into the water" (17:15). Mark adds more details. The father also said, "He can't talk because he is possessed by a demon ... The demon often makes him fall into the fire or into water to kill him" (Mark 9:17, 22). Jesus identified the evil spirit and exorcised it (9:25-27).

This demon, a particularly violent and tenacious one, demonstrates how completely a demon can control a person. Dr. L. R. Curtis, a nationally known newspaper columnist, quotes the words of a mother who had consulted him for help regarding the vicious and even violent treatment she gave her baby. She lamented, "I can't control myself. It's like I'm possessed with an evil spirit." Is this possible? The Bible says it is.

In his statement on the devil and demon possession, Pope Paul VI stressed that one of the great gaps in modern therapy is the failure to analyze what is really wrong with people. He laments that this matter of demon possession "is given little attention today, though it should be studied again. Some people think a sufficient compensation can be found in psychoanalytical and psychiatric studies." In fact the real cause may be occupation of the faculties by Satan.

No one knows how many people today are demon possessed. But I'm convinced many North Americans are demon possessed, though their problems are diagnosed as something else altogether. I am also convinced the number is increasing rapidly.

Take the current staggering increase in crime. One in three Americans say he has been a victim of a crime in the last year. When he was running for the presidency, George McGovern lamented, "The stain of violence stains our time again. It is a recurring nightmare which shadows our brief years together as human beings." What difference is there between our times and a statement like this—"Two men ... lived in a cemetery and were so dangerous that no one could go through that area" (Matthew 8:28)?

Thousands have nothing organically wrong with them, but they feel, as one woman puts it, "perpetually on the rim of a canyon." Looking over her shoulder, this woman bemoaned, "There's just no one to talk to, and I'm going absolutely mad." She says that she is representative of many Americans.

It is only one step from demonic depression to demon possession which explodes into the kind of crime which we are reading about more and more today. People recently charged with murder in Montana and in California not only readily admitted the murders, but described in gory details how they had dismembered their victims as part of a satanic ritual. In Michigan, a seventeen-year-old girl was tortured and slain, and those charged with the killing claimed openly to be "Satan's satanic servants." In New Jersey, newspapers report that a man was killed so he could return to earth as leader of "forty leagues of demons."

Satan's manifestations by no means consist only of demon possession. He may intellectually sophisticate a man and completely blind his mind to God. Paul wrote to the Corinthians, "The god of this world [Satan] hath blinded the minds of them which believe not, lest the light of the glorious gospel of Christ, who is the image of God, should shine unto them" (2 Corinthians 4:4, KJV). The words of a pop song say, "The whole world is blind."

The reason why many of the world's great scientific and philosophic minds are often militantly anti-Christ is "because the carnal mind is enmity against God: for it is not subject to the law of God, neither indeed can be" (Romans 8:7, KJV). In fact, a mind biased against God by the devil cannot be changed apart from spiritual rebirth. In Revelation we read of men who simply "would not renounce their demon worship... Neither did they change their mind and attitude" (9:20, 21). An example of this trend can already be seen in the popularity of novels like Herman Hesse's *Siddharthas,* which takes its myriads of readers on trips from the facts of God to the fictions of Satan.

One of the guests on a *Mike Douglas Show,* Professor Hans Holzer, avowed that certain strange activities had been photographed. A huge chest of drawers, which would have required four men to lift, was hoisted and moved across part of a room and up onto a bed. The act was induced by a spiritist medium, who also had the "spirit" take a small dog from the living room floor and set it down on the roof of the house.

Many people have taken up the hobby of photographing and tape recording ghost figures, and spirit voices and sounds. This is so popular that you might open the most scholarly or fashionable magazine or newspaper and see pictures and articles on "finds," or hear the voices on television or radio. But do these spirits actually speak? Of course they do. As Jesus ministered, demons "came out ... shouting" (Luke 4:41). Curious people today want to hear them speak, and then are terrified (or falsely comforted) when they do.

THE DEVIL

In an extremely fashionable residential area of Long Island, a mansion belonging to Jackie Onassis' aunt and cousin is supposedly haunted by three ghosts. The medieval Abbey in the village of Beaulier in southern England is allegedly occupied by ghosts which Lady Montagu, mistress of the estate, says everyone simply takes for granted.

While most people claim to have no serious interest in the devil and demons, others are specialists in working in harmony with demons—witches, wizards, and warlocks. These are females and males who so give themselves to the devil that they are able to communicate with him or his demons. They trust him and he "trusts" them.

Is there a basis in fact for communication with the spirit world? Does it take place through a medium? King Saul of Israel once consulted a medium (1 Samuel 28). People still do. *Time* magazine, in its review of *The Rainbird Pattern* by Victor Canning, which deals with the exploits of a modern medium, states that "a spirit world flickers on the edges" of a great number of people today, to which they gravitate "like a drunk motorist drifting off the road." This, perhaps, is the only explanation for people flocking to see movies like Orson Welles's *The Devil-God* with its subtitle, "Enter the occult world," and see the "terror and shock of exorcism, witchcraft, and necromancy!"

People are chronic worshipers. Karl Jung, one of the pioneers of modern psychology, and the great Russian writer Dostoyevsky have noted this. Jesus said it. To the Samaritan woman he observed, "Ye worship ye know not what" (John 4:22, KJV). Except for those who worship God in truth, "all people will walk every one in the name of his god" (Micah 4:5, KJV). And the consequence is that all people who do not worship the true God give their allegiance to the devil.

Paul taught this. Among the Athenians, the philosophical elite of that day, Paul "was deeply troubled by all the idols he saw everywhere throughout the city" (Acts 17:16). He saw Athens as a "city wholly given to idolatry" (v. 16, KJV). Though Athenians were perhaps the most learned people in history, when it came to their spiritual lives, he said, they "ignorantly worship" (v. 23, KJV). To nearby Corinth, he stated that offering prayers and allegiance to idols was an act of giving oneself "to devils, and not to God: and I would not that ye should have fellowship with devils" (1 Corinthians 10:20, KJV). So Paul implores and warns them, "my dearly beloved, flee from idolatry" (v. 14). These ancient Greeks, whether ignorantly like the Athenians or knowingly like the Corinthians, worshiped false gods, and as such were demon worshipers. It is still true that whether a person is an illiterate or an intellectual, a pagan or a nominal Christian, if he is not worshiping the true God, he is worshiping demons.

Today our idols may not be images, but millions of people care more about cars, houses, and bank accounts than they do about God. These items then become idols.

Satan also manifests himself to man through religious imitators of the true God. The devil has never really been very original. He was created to be an engineer, not an architect; an administrator, not a creator of new ideas. So he apes what he observes God doing. Like God, he wants to be worshiped, so he even asked Jesus "to fall down and worship me" (Matthew 4:9, KJV).

Here is an absolutely amazing fact—Jesus taught that Satan so gets his followers into his grip that they actually cast out demons. "At the Judgment many will tell me, 'Lord, Lord, we told others about you and used your name to cast out demons and to do many other great miracles.' But I will reply, 'You have never been mine. Go away, for your deeds are evil' '' (Matthew 7:22, 23). These religionists—who had postured as Christians, even casting out demons—not having been born again at all, were all the time children of the devil; and they actually cast out demons! It sounds incredible, but it demonstrates what an ingenious religionist and imitator of God Satan really is. Nor is it the only instance of this in the Gospels. Jesus plainly told the Pharisees, "You are the children of your father the devil" (John 8:44). But he also said, "What about your own followers? For they cast out demons!"—proof that Satan's "kingdom is filled with civil war [and] is doomed" (Luke 11:19, 17). This may astonish us. It did not amaze Paul. To the Corinthians he wrote, "I am not surprised! Satan can change himself into an angel of light, so it is no wonder his servants can do it too, and seem like godly ministers" (2 Corinthians 11:14, 15).

An actual instance of non-Christians, children of the devil, casting out demons—and this to their own peril—is recorded in Acts. Luke describes how "a team of itinerant Jews who were traveling from town to town casting out demons planned to experiment by using the name of the Lord Jesus. The incantation they decided on was this: 'I adjure you by Jesus, whom Paul preaches, to come out!' Seven sons of Sceva, a Jewish priest, were doing this. But when they tried it on a man possessed by a demon, the demon replied, 'I know Jesus and I know Paul, but who are you?' And he leaped on two of them and beat them up, so that they fled out of his house naked and badly injured. The story of what happened spread quickly all through Ephesus, to Jews and Greeks alike; and a solemn fear descended on the city, and the name of the Lord Jesus was greatly honored" (Acts 19:13-17).

You understandably may ask: But the devil does so many nice, good, and legal things—how can he do good and yet be the devil? In the same way that the Mafia can allegedly do fifty billion dollars worth of business in the United States annually, most of it, as it appears to the public, conducted in a very legal and "straight" way. Yes, because that's what works best for the aggrandizement of the world's most vile crime syndicate. So the devil. It's greatly to his advantage if he can pose as a good guy and so get his followers to give him loyal, undeviating allegiance. The Bible says that in the end they will all be damned.

Magic is the practice of ritual for the purpose of bringing demonic forces to bear on an individual, a group of people, or a human situation. The practice of black magic invokes Satan's powers for purposes of vengeance, reprisal, intimidation, or persecution, and is for the sheer gratification of evil desire.

God forbade his followers to practice black magic (Deuteronomy 18:10). In Acts 19, we read that many of the Ephesians "had been practicing black magic" (vv. 18, 19), and by so doing were holding a sort of sword of Damocles over people. When the gospel set those people free, they burned their articles for practicing black magic.

Today we can read newspaper reports of magic nearly every week. The mayor of Calgary, Alberta, asks an Indian chieftain to lift the curse he put on that city. A Mayo Clinic patient spends a long time in effective and hopeful therapy, only to go home and die because a voodooist curses him and robs him of the will to live. A Londoner claims that actress Jayne Mansfield was killed in an automobile accident in 1967 because a black magic curse had lowered the boom on her life. A front-page headline in *The Toronto*

Star reads: "NIAGRA FALLS 'WITCH' ORDERED TO RETURN FEE FOR LIFTING CURSE." An article follows, detailing the terror of a family when a curse was pronounced on them, and the fact that a very large sum of money was paid for the lifting of the curse.

The universal revival of black magic is evident. We are told that in the United States there is a practicing witch for every two clergymen, while in England and Germany the number of practicing witches may outnumber the clergy.

Throughout history the rituals of *bona fide* magicians have differed, but the evil principles involved have not changed much. The Black Mass of the medieval era was a sort of forerunner of modern black magic. In the Black Mass Satan is substituted for God, evil for good; the altar is a naked female; the consecrated wine is replaced by the blood of children or animals slain for this purpose, or by urine. Instead of being conducted at the beginning of daylight, it is held at night. Halloween replaces Christmas as the annual festival event. Orgies and acts of gross sexual perversion replace an ordered and reverent atmosphere.

What is white magic? It is the use of magic for purposes of purportedly helping people. After all, say its patrons, man is in a state of helpless, hopeless confusion, guilt, fear, boredom, and despair. To alleviate these pressures, he needs spiritual escape and occupation.

This is true. But white magic is not the way to go about it. Using white magic to try to iron out the bugaboos of life is at best a pseudo-sedative and in truth is an example of an immoral attitude described by Paul: "our sins serve a good purpose" (Romans 3:5).

There are always those who will argue that we are to "give the devil his due," and if we can get some white

magic help from the devil, we should take it. The devil
is clever. He will give a person help if it will draw
that individual to his corner and keep him coming his
way. But the Lord warns his people that under no
circumstances are they to "call on the evil spirits for
aid... Anyone doing these things is an object of horror
and disgust" to him (Deuteronomy 18:10, 12).

Open up the *Los Angeles Times* and you can read of
how a psychic expert, possessing occult awareness,
can unveil mysteries which will ensure "good luck
cycles with cosmic powers," and the outcome will be
health, wealth, and success. Or there is Londoner Janet
Augustin, the "friendly neighborhood witch" who
works white magic for her friends in the stock market.
The devil is well acquainted with the promo slogan,
"There's nothing that succeeds like success."

For a comparison of the abilities of God's people
and the practitioners of white magic, we can read of
King Nebuchadnezzar's engagement of Daniel,
Hananiah, Mishael, and Azariah, four of the king's
regular staff advisors. "And in all matters requiring
information and balanced judgment, the king found
these young men's advice ten times better than that
of all the skilled magicians and wise astrologers in his
realm" (Daniel 1:19, 20).

Why were Daniel and the Hebrew youths more
effective than the pagan magicians? The answer is
twofold. First, Satan does not know the future, nor can
he do all things. God does know everything—and he
can do anything. Second, Satan is a deceiver, and
he and his demons slip the expedient answer to his
agents—not necessarily the truthful answer. Satan
evidently sizes up a situation, weighing what he thinks
will be most advantageous to his cause, and
accordingly communicates his message.

Astrology, and the whole basis and evolution of

horoscopes, have come down to modern man from ancient Babylon, as the Ten Commandments have come down to us from ancient Israel.

On what basis do we link ancient astrology with Satan and demon worship? It is made clear in Isaiah 47: "O Babylon ... bragging as the greatest in the world—listen to the sentence of my court upon your sins ... there will be no atonement then to cleanse away your sins. Call out the demon hordes you've worshiped all these years. You have advisors by the ton—your astrologers and stargazers, who try to tell you what the future holds. But they are as useless as dried grass burning in the fire. They cannot even deliver themselves! You'll get no help from them at all. Theirs is no fire to sit beside to make you warm" (vv. 1, 8-14).

Today the impact of the horoscope is nearly unbelievable. Ninety million Americans believe astrology is a credible guide. Six million Americans say they plan each day on the basis of what they read in their morning horoscopes. Of the 1,700 daily newspapers, 1,300 carry horoscopes, and editors say that the horoscope is one of the most popular sections of their papers. Talk shows conducted by astrologers are on television and radio. A front-running Democratic presidential hopeful decided to drop out of the race when in his horoscope he got the message that he should do so. In Canada, a New Democrat was reported to have based his hopes of winning a recent Canadian federal election on the fact that he "recently visited a Toronto clairvoyant and astrologer who told him he was definitely going to win." Some well-known people, such as British playboy Michael Pearson, publicize the fact that the most important guiding force in their lives is their horoscope. This is true of an astonishingly high percentage of people in the entertainment industry.

A highly sophisticated magazine announced the invention of a completely "computerized astrology" which gives "millions of people" a "personal" authentic forecast of their future, containing "14,000 words, a whole book about you and you alone."

Johnny Carson of "The Tonight Show" asked what it is that is making people turn with such slavish dependence, and in such large numbers, to horoscopes for guidance. We think it is because man wants and needs a higher power. Astrology offers to meet that need.

We might also ask, Why are so many horoscope predictions generally accurate? One reason is because horoscopes tend to predict what seems most probable. Another reason is that while Satan does not know much of the future—this accounts for the incredibly high percentage of mispredictions horoscope followers tolerate—he is indeed very clever. Intelligent and powerful, he is able to attain a much higher number of correct projections than men who have so much less knowledge and technique at their disposal.

Are there ever circumstances in which a Christian is entitled to look to the stars for spiritual guidance? No! The Christian is not to look to the stars, but beyond them, just as a wife is not to settle her affection on the sparkling jewelry, but on the husband who bought it for her as an expression of his love. Moses warned the Israelites, "Do not look up into the sky to worship the sun, moon, or stars" (Deuteronomy 4:19). This, Moses said, violates the people's "covenant with God" (17:2). As God's people today, we are not to look to the heavens for spiritual guidance.

Do not, however, confuse astrology with

astronomy or astrophysics. The Bible makes a clear distinction between the two. The latter is God's work (Psalm 19:1); the former is a tool of the devil. According to a petition released to the public in late 1975 by 186 astronomers, astrophysicists, and scientists in related fields—eighteen Nobel Prize winners among them—the 5,000 American astrologers are making an extortionate living off the public and are doing so without any proven scientific validity whatsoever. Endeavoring to call a halt to their activities, this concerned body asked the public to challenge the astrologers' pretentious claims, avowing that they are all astrological charlatans.

Astrology engages the zodiac and the horoscope as a medium of communication between Satan's kingdom and his human children. Other means of his communication are the Ouija board, palmistry, tarot cards, and such practices as reading the intestines of certain animals. This manifestation of the devil, while closely related to witchcraft, sorcery, and magic, is often called divination—a prying into the future. Another name, of course, is fortune-telling.

The Bible mentions some items which are parallels to modern methods of discerning the future. A silver drinking cup was used in ancient Egypt for fortune-telling (Genesis 44:5). If the ancients didn't know what to do, they would call their magicians to use divination. Perhaps they would cast lots by shaking arrows from the quiver, or sacrifice to idols and inspect the liver of their sacrifice. It seems incredible, but this practice in divination and fortune-telling is being practiced widely today, not only in Asia, Africa, South America, and the Island world, but also in North America and Europe. The practice is coming to be known as psychometry. Psychometrists profess to read the future by consulting certain objects which react in certain ways and convey certain messages. A major league baseball team, desiring to win a world championship, consulted crystal balls and tea leaves to see if there was a triumph in their future. There wasn't!

Ouija boards and tea leaves are often used by fortune-tellers to tell the future of a seeker. This kind of thing has gone on for thousands of years. Through the prophet Hosea God said, "Wine, women, and song have robbed my people of their brains. For they are asking a piece of wood to tell them what to do. 'Divine Truth' comes to them through tea leaves! Longing after idols has made them foolish. For they have played the harlot, serving other gods, deserting me. They sacrifice to idols on the tops of mountains; they go up into the hills to burn incense in the pleasant shade of oaks and poplars and terebinth trees" (Hosea 4:11-13).

How history repeats itself! Ancient Israel couldn't think clearly because of their dissipation and moral corruption. They had lost contact with God, so they turned to Satan's kingdom and wooden instruments and tea leaves—anything that would work. Some people may argue that there is really no harm in being or going to a fortune-teller. Jeane Dixon is such a nice, honorable, and religious person! But what does the Bible say? Sybil Leek or Louise Huebner is so often right. But what does the Bible say? That is our criterion. That is our guide.

Many of us have seen films or read descriptions of people walking through fire or up the red-hot rungs of a ladder without being burned. As Satan duplicated some of Moses' and Aaron's first miracles in Egypt, it also seems that he can duplicate God's protection of Shadrach, Meshach, and Abednego as they walked in the furnace.

THE DEVIL

The *Cleveland Plain Dealer Sunday Magazine,* in July 1972, carried a documented story by a highly reputable reporter who said, "I have seen a man, in the presence of medical witnesses, chew up a light bulb and swallow it, stick a sharpened bicycle spoke through one side of his face and out the other, and walk on a fire fed by kerosene—all without serious visible harm.... Every four years in Penang, Malaysia, a metal ladder about twenty-five feet high is erected in one of the town squares. There are seventeen rungs in the ladder, each one a steel bar honed to the sharpness of a razor blade. To test this, a spectator gently laid a banana on one of the lower rungs; it was almost sliced in two by its own weight. When everything is ready, the performers appear. They are male mediums of the Taoist religion.... Before the ceremony begins the mediums induce a trance by inhaling opium fumes. To try to ascend the Ladder of Swords without putting themselves into a trance would have fatal consequences, they insist. When they are entranced—a state in which, glassy-eyed, they appear oblivious of their surroundings—the mediums ... slowly but deliberately climb to the top and then down again. Astonishingly, none is injured in any way—not even a scratch."

People ask, How can it be? The devil does it! And it's coming to North America. *The Los Angeles Times* reports that such things are allegedly being done in a California theater: "a powerful devil rite" with "the dancers of Mali."

We will never stand up and level with the devil until we realize that he exists and is ever endeavoring to use, not the most conspicuous, but the most effective means of manifesting himself. Often he's most effective if he is as inconspicuous as possible. But you can be sure of this—the devil believes that the end justifies the means.

CHAPTER SEVEN

The Devil and His War Effort

Satan is not only sinister and incorrigible; but he is also a master strategist. His objectives are not only unequaled for their evil intent, but are executed with precision and ruthlessness which would make today's mobsters look like kindergarten kiddies playing cops and robbers. He is the super-godfather with some longstanding goals which he is determined to achieve at any cost. He keeps his vast array of troops mobilized; he has a program.

The devil's objectives are based in his sworn enmity against Jesus Christ. Back in the Garden of Eden, when Eve hurtled the human race into rebellion against the Creator, God answered Satan's declaration of war. "From now on," he declared, "you and the woman will be enemies, as will all of your offspring and hers.... He [Jesus Christ] shall strike you on your head, while you will strike at his heel" (Genesis 3:15). The die had been cast. It was Satan the Enemy versus Christ the Redeemer.

During his earthly ministry, Jesus let it be know that he would eventually overthrow Satan and his kingdom. Indeed, Jesus began the offensive when he was here on earth. He announced, "But if I am casting out demons because of power from God, it proves that the Kingdom of God has arrived. For when Satan, strong and fully armed, guards his palace it is safe—until someone stronger and better-armed attacks and overcomes him and strips him of his weapons and carries off his belongings. Anyone who is not for me is against me; if he isn't helping me, he is hurting my cause" (Luke 11:20-23).

As we have seen, our Lord frequently encountered the members of the kingdom of darkness. In Capernaum, for example, as "he was teaching in the synagogue, a man possessed by a demon began shouting at Jesus, 'Go away! We want nothing to do with you, Jesus from Nazareth. You have come to destroy us. I know who you are—the Holy Son of God.' Jesus cut him short. 'Be silent!' he told the demon. 'Come out!' The demon threw the man to the floor as the crowd watched, and then left him without hurting him further" (Luke 4:33-35).

By the Sea of Galilee "a man ... came to meet him, a man who had been demon-possessed for a long time... As soon as he saw Jesus he shrieked and fell to the ground before him, screaming, 'What do you want with me, Jesus, Son of God Most High? Please, I beg you, oh, don't torment me!' For Jesus was already commanding the demon to leave him" (Luke 8:27, 28).

As Jesus freed people from Satan's grip, some religious leaders observed his miracles and rationalized that " 'he can cast out demons because he is Satan, king of devils.' Jesus knew their thoughts and

replied, 'A divided kingdom ends in ruin. A city or
home divided against itself cannot stand. And if Satan is
casting out Satan, he is fighting himself, and
destroying his own kingdom. And if, as you claim, I
am casting out demons by invoking the powers of
Satan, then what power do your own people use when
they cast them out? Let them answer your accusation!
But if I am casting out demons by the Spirit of God,
then the Kingdom of God has arrived among you. One
cannot rob Satan's kingdom without first binding
Satan. Only then can his demons be cast out!' ''
(Matthew 12:24-30).

Satan's goal to dethrone Jesus reached its climax at
the cross. The inner turmoil of Jesus' thoughts are
unveiled in a prophetic psalm: "The enemy, this gang
of evil men, circles me like a pack of dogs; they have
pierced my hands and feet" (Psalm 22:16). It was a
desperate, frantic effort to do away with Jesus
forever by ending his life on that cross.

But it was Satan himself who was being vanquished.
The Son of God had become "flesh and blood ... born
in human form; for only as a human being could he die
and in dying break the power of the devil who had the
power of death. Only in that way could he deliver
those who through fear of death have been living all
their lives as slaves to constant dread. We all know he
did not come as an angel but as a human being"
(Hebrews 2:14-16). Only as we understand this can we
understand how desperate Satan must have been. But
what at first seemed like a defeat for the forces of God
was God's greatest victory! And though we don't
yet see Christ's vindication, when all things will be
put under his rule, personal redemption is available to
all believers in Christ.

It is understandable that Satan, having had to
concede victory to Jesus, should now be determined to

keep people away from Jesus. Rowland Hill, one of England's great preachers in the eighteenth century, was walking down the street one day when he saw a drove of pigs following a man. "This," said Hill, "excited my curiosity so much that I determined to follow. I did so and to my great surprise, I saw them follow him to the slaughterhouse. I said to the man, 'My friend, how did you induce the pigs to follow you here?' He replied, 'I had a basket of beans under my arm, and I dropped a few as I came along, and so they followed me.' And so it is that Satan has the basket of beans under his arm; and he drops them as he goes along, and what multitudes he induces to follow him to an everlasting slaughterhouse!" Paul wrote that "if the Good News we preach is hidden to anyone, it is hidden from the one who is on the road to eternal death" (2 Corinthians 4:3).

Take, for example, the Pharisees, devout believers whose very religious existence centered in the coming Messiah. But when John the Baptist came as Christ's forerunner to announce, "See! There is the Lamb of God!" (John 1:36), what did they do? They had a mental block and said of John, "He has a demon!" (Matthew 11:18, KJV). And when Jesus began performing miracles and proclaiming his good news of hope, some of them became insane with fury. " 'You Samaritan! Foreigner! Devil!' the Jewish leaders snarled. 'Didn't we say all along you were possessed by a demon?' 'No,' Jesus said, 'I have no demon in me...' " Whereupon the religious leaders said, "Now we know you are possessed by a demon!" (John 8:48, 52). They were so deluded by the devil that they just couldn't accept Jesus of Nazareth as the promised Messiah. They were victims of a supernatural spell, put on them by the devil.

Keeping people in a state of spiritual "lostness" is a

paramount objective of the devil which he never ceases pursuing. I never preach the gospel anywhere in the world, whether in a crusade, on radio, on television, or through other means, but that I am aware that Satan is fighting, tooth and nail. If the Word gets out, Satan seeks to squelch it; and if it reaches the hearers, viewers, or readers, he brings out the weapons in his vile arsenal to try to keep people from Christ. When I preach, I am in a supernatural battle for the minds and hearts of my listeners. Some can listen, but because of Satan they cannot "hear."

Jesus made this clear in one of his most familiar parables. He compared the preacher of the Word to a sower who distributes seed. "The hard path where some seed fell represents the hard hearts of those who hear the words of God, but then the devil comes and steals the words away and prevents people from believing and being saved" (Luke 8:12). Every time a preacher of the gospel stands up to present Christ to unconverted people, he can be sure Satan will be there.

In another parable, Jesus tells the story of a farmer who sowed seed in his field, and one night his enemy sowed weeds in the field. Jesus explained, "I am the farmer who sows the choice seed. The field is the world, and the seed represents the people of the Kingdom; the thistles are the people belonging to Satan. The enemy who sowed the thistles among the wheat is the devil" (Matthew 13:37-39). Here it is clear that the devil constantly tries to choke out the beginnings of spiritual life.

Perhaps the most dramatic account of Satan's efforts to keep an individual in his kingdom is recorded in Acts 13. Paul and Barnabas had just been ordained to the ministry in Antioch and were on their first evangelistic tour. They had reached the island of Cyprus and the governor, Sergius Paulus, "invited

THE DEVIL

Paul and Barnabas to visit him, for he wanted to hear
their message from God. But the sorcerer, Elymas (his
name in Greek), interfered and urged the governor to
pay no attention to what Paul and Barnabas said, trying
to keep him from trusting the Lord. Then Paul, filled
with the Holy Spirit, glared angrily at the sorcerer
and said, 'You son of the devil, full of every sort of
trickery and villainy, enemy of all that is good, will you
never end your opposition to the Lord? And now God
has laid his hand of punishment upon you, and you will
be stricken awhile with blindness.' Instantly mist and
darkness fell upon him, and he began wandering
around begging for someone to take his hand and
lead him'' (vv. 7-11).

A whole people can be thus spiritually blinded. A
sociologist reported that a sect in a wild and desolate area
of Asia Minor practices a diabolical perversion of
Christianity, introduced to them by an outcast monk
who passed through that region on muleback during
the Crusades. To this day, they worship the powers
of darkness, honor their brigands, reward their
ne'er-do-wells, and build shrines to the devil.

Of one thing we can always be sure: the devil blankets
his disciples with darkness. And if you as a Christian
share your faith with an unbeliever, the devil will do his
best to divert the one to whom you are witnessing.

Another of Satan's objectives high on his priority
list is a relentless effort to discredit or corrupt the
written Word of God. In fact, the devil has inspired his
worshipers today to publish a *Satan Bible*. This is one
example of how it perverts Jesus' words: "Blessed are
the strong, for they shall possess the earth. If a man
smites you on one cheek, smite him on the other."
Satan will also try to corrupt the Word of God by
twisting it or quoting it completely out of context.
Shakespeare aptly wrote in *The Merchant of Venice,*

"The devil can cite Scripture for his purpose."

In about A.D. 1800 the carriers of the gospel message began to take the Word to the world in an unprecedented way. But during the last century the devil seems to have stepped up his efforts to damage the integrity of the Bible. His hammers have worn flat and are broken on the anvil of impregnable Scripture (as Gladstone observed), but his pounding has wrought untold havoc. Many of the great battles in the church today are being fought over the Word of God.

Often we blame the radical-liberal or modernist of this century, the German higher critics of the last century, or the French rationalists of the eighteenth century for undermining the Scriptures. This is a shallow reading of history. The questioning and corrupting of the Word of God has been a trick of the devil long predating Paul's lament over those who "corrupt the word of God" (2 Corinthians 2:17, KJV) or even King Jehoiakim's carving pieces out of the Old Testament Scriptures with a penknife (Jeremiah 36:23). It began in the Garden of Eden when Satan asked Eve, "Yea, hath God said?" (Genesis, 3:1, KJV).

Jesus said that when his Word was proclaimed, "the fowls of the air came and devoured it up" (Mark 4:4, KJV). Later he explained that these birds were the devil at work (v. 15), preventing the Word from germinating in the hearts of potential believers.

If the devil fails to drive a wedge between a man and the Word of God, he has another trick up his sleeve. It is his accusation of Christians—he is called "the Accuser of our brothers" (Revelation 12:10). So preoccupied is he that "he accused them day and night before our God."

The devil's opposition, as Paul wrote to Timothy, can really get to a believer. In fact, the pastor of a church, Paul explained, "must be well spoken of by

113

people outside the church—those who aren't Christians—so that Satan can't trip him with many accusations, and leave him without freedom to lead his flock" (1 Timothy 3:6, 7).

One of the devil's delights is to encourage gossipping and quarreling among believers. These are two of the fastest ways on record to split or splinter a church and destroy its effectiveness. Jesus had said that "by this shall all men know that ye are my disciples, if ye have love one to another" (John 13:35, KJV). The Apostle Paul exhorted, "Love Christians everywhere" (1 Peter 2:17).

But often our tongues get in the way of our love. The fire that sets our tongues aflame with accusations and quarrelings is fed by hell. In his well-known description of the power of the tongue, James wrote, "Dear brothers, don't be too eager to tell others their faults, for we all make many mistakes; and when we teachers of religion, who should know better, do wrong, our punishment will be greater than it would be for others. If anyone can control his tongue, it proves that he has perfect control over himself in every other way. We can make a large horse turn around and go wherever we want to by means of a small bit in his mouth. And a tiny rudder makes a huge ship turn wherever the pilot wants it to go, even though the winds are strong. So also the tongue is a small thing, but what enormous damage it can do. A great forest can be set on fire by one tiny spark. And the tongue is a flame of fire. It is full of wickedness and poisons every part of the body. And the tongue is set on fire by hell itself, and can turn our whole lives into a blazing flame of destruction and disaster" (3:1-6).

The devil loves loose tongues. James candidly stated that "men have trained, or can train, every kind of animal or bird that lives and every kind of reptile and fish, but no human being can tame the tongue. It is always ready to pour out its deadly poison. Sometimes it praises our heavenly Father, and sometimes it breaks out into curses against men who are made like God. And so blessing and cursing come pouring out of the same mouth. Dear brothers, surely this is not right" (3:7-10).

When members of the church declare war on each other, the devil declares himself neutral, then gives ammunition to both sides. The untold damage which loose tongues in the church have done through the centuries is incalculable. Many Christians are like vacuum cleaners—they suck in all the dirt they can find, and then they make a lot of noise. Adlai Stevenson once said that when you throw mud, you lose ground. Scorpions eject poison with their tails, people with their tongues. Too many churches are like the island off the coast of Maine where the people proverbially make their living by taking in each other's washing. The most gossipy woman in a certain church came forward one night during a revival, crying, "Pastor, I want to put my tongue on the altar." But the pastor had been bitten by her too many times and he replied, "Sorry, sister, not here! This altar is not long enough for your tongue!"

Just before the Battle of Trafalgar, Lord Nelson summoned Admiral Collingwood and Captain Rotherham because he had heard that they were not on good terms with each other. He placed their hands together and looking them both in the face, gestured toward the force with whom they battled. Sharply he exhorted, "Look! Yonder is your enemy!" They got the message. Sometimes I wonder if the shortest road to revival would not be for our Lord to take all of us in his church aside, rebuke our petty quarreling, point to the devil and his kingdom, and exhort, "Look! Yonder is

your enemy!'' We are to be responsible to Christ,
the Head of the church; we are not called to spend
our time looking at what other Christians are doing
wrong.

Another of Satan's objectives is to defeat believers
in their efforts to live the Christian life. Paul wrote to
the Ephesians that they were involved in spiritual
warfare and that "in every battle you will need faith
as your shield to stop the fiery arrows aimed at you
by Satan" (6:16).

Satan succeeded in defeating Peter. When our Lord
was approaching the cross, he turned abruptly to
Peter, to whom he had entrusted the special keys of the
Kingdom (Matthew 16:19) and said, "Simon, Simon,
Satan has asked to have you, to sift you like
wheat." Peter's impulsive nature guided his answer,
"Lord, I am ready to go to jail with you, and even to die
with you." He sounded brave and true. But things
happened just as our Lord had predicted and Satan
had determined. Jesus had said, "Peter, let me tell you
something. Between now and tomorrow morning
when the rooster crows, you will deny me three
times, declaring that you don't even know me"
(Luke 22:31-34; cf. vv. 55-62). Peter's experience is
reenacted all around us, and in us. We must exercise
strong, growing faith. We must take a firm stand. We
are indeed on a battlefield, not a playground.

A defeated Christian is a silenced witness, in whom the
devil delights. Here is another of Satan's leading
objectives: to destroy the testimony of the gospel. The
Apostle Paul wrote to the Thessalonians how "we
wanted very much to come and I, Paul, tried again
and again, but Satan stopped us" (1 Thessalonians
2:18). As a preacher of the gospel, I have experienced
some of this opposition which Paul knew when he set out
to share Christ with his contemporaries. It is

important, of course, to discern between what may not
be the will of God, and what may be barriers erected
by Satan. This is one of the reasons why we must
walk in the Spirit and know the guidings and
providings of the Lord. I am convinced that huge
numbers of people are without the Word and the gospel
because God-directed evangels ran into opposition
from the devil as Paul did, and gave up the battle.

In many parts of the world today it is illegal to share
the gospel of Christ with other members of society.
Those who witness take the risk of being imprisoned
or even executed. Who is responsible for this? The
devil! Satan has never hesitated to concentrate his forces
on having witnesses persecuted. It is all a part of what
the Bible prophesied would happen: "The devil will
soon throw some of you into prison" (Revelation
2:10).

Ironically, Satan's persecution, torture, and
imprisonment of believers is going to be turned on him
in the future. He will be thrown into the "Lake of Fire
burning with sulphur where the Creature and False
Prophet are, and they will be tormented day and night
forever and ever" (Revelation 20:10). Knowing this is
his sentence, Satan wants to take as many people
with him to hell as he can, to share with him and his
demons the torments of the damned. The Apostle John
noted, "I saw a great white throne and the one who sat
upon it, from whose face the earth and sky fled away,
but they found no place to hide. I saw the dead, great
and small, standing before God; and the Books were
opened, including the Book of Life. And the dead
were judged according to the things written in The
Books, each according to the deeds he had done. The
oceans surrendered the bodies buried in them; and the
earth and the underworld gave up the dead in them.
Each was judged according to his deeds. And Death and

Hell were thrown into the Lake of Fire. This is the Second Death—the Lake of Fire. And if anyone's name was not found recorded in the Book of Life, he was thrown into the Lake of Fire" (Revelation 20:11-15).

Many people have told me that they could not believe in a God who would prepare such a place as hell for human beings. But Jesus made it clear that heaven, not hell, was the place God wanted men to go. Indeed, he said that he himself would be going directly from this earth to heaven to prepare a place of many mansions for his redeemed (John 14:2, 3). God did not really make hell for human beings; he made it for the devil and his demons. A person's own refusal of Christ sends him to hell. Jesus said that at the judgment, "I will turn to those on my left and say, 'Away with you, you cursed ones, into the eternal fire prepared for the devil and his demons' " (Matthew 25:41).

So the devil's greatest wish is to arrange reservations for you in hell. Demons are delegated by Satan to coax, cajole, and push unredeemed, unregenerate people into the Lake of Fire. When Jesus was here on earth, he cast a legion of demons out of a man and promptly "they left the man and went into the pigs [2,000 of them], and immediately the whole herd rushed down the mountainside and fell over a cliff into the lake below" (Luke 8:33). Today demons are obsessing and rushing human beings over the precipice of impenitence into hell.

Who will be lost with the devil and his demons? They are "the cowards who turn back from following me, and those who are unfaithful to me, and the corrupt, and murderers, and the immoral, and those conversing with demons, and idol worshipers and all liars—their doom is in the Lake that burns with fire and sulphur.

This is the Second Death" (Revelation 21:8).

There is always a note of sobriety in last words.
The Bible concludes with an entreaty: "The Spirit and
the bride say, 'Come.' Let each one who hears them
say the same, 'Come.' Let the thirsty one
come—anyone who wants to; let him come and drink
the Water of Life without charge" (Revelation 22:16).
But preceding this glorious, final invitation is the
comparably sober pronouncement: "Outside the city
are those who have strayed away from God, and the
sorcerers and the immoral and murderers and idolaters,
and all who love to lie, and do so" (v. 15).

CHAPTER EIGHT

The Devil's Devices

It is one thing to have objectives. It is quite another to have the skills to execute those objectives. The devil not only has a program of total evil, he is a skilled technician who plans his work and works his plan. Being aware of his techniques is essential to our overcoming his influence in our everyday lives.

PRIDE

God has always hated pride. Solomon said, "These six things doth the Lord hate; yea, seven are an abomination unto him." And heading the list is "a proud look" (Proverbs 6:16, 17, KJV). Solomon warned us, "Pride goes before destruction and haughtiness before a fall. Better poor and humble than proud and rich" (Proverbs 16:18, 19). Jesus said that pride is a "vile thing" (Mark 7:22, 23). "Pride," wrote the Apostle John, is "... not from God" (1 John 2:16).

It is impossible for a person to please God or merit his mercy as long as he persists in his pride. The Apostle Peter said, "God gives special blessings to those who are humble, but sets himself against those who are proud. If you will humble yourselves under the mighty hand of God, in his good time he will lift you up... Be careful—watch out for attacks from Satan, your great enemy" (1 Peter 5:5, 6, 8). Genuine humility comes from the Spirit of Christ. But whenever a believer feels a surge of pride, consciousness of haughtiness or arrogance, an inflated sensation of his own importance or indispensability, he can be sure of one thing: the devil is near.

Pride is a strange illness—it makes everyone sick but the one who has it.

TEMPTATION

At the outset of history, Satan tempted Eve and the consequence to the human race was sin—the greatest tragedy of all time. Rudyard Kipling once wrote, "The devil whispered behind the leaves, 'It's pretty.' " Temptation was also the weapon with which the devil tried to overcome Jesus (Matthew 4:1-11). Our Lord was the only person to ever utterly resist Satan's temptation. This is the reason he could invite us to pray, "Don't bring us into temptation, but deliver us from the Evil One" (Matthew 6:13).

Sooner or later all of us face temptation from the devil and his demons. But the Apostle Paul assures us that "no temptation is irresistible. You can trust God to keep the temptation from becoming so strong that you can't stand against it, for he has promised this and will do what he says. He will show you how to escape temptation's power so that you can bear up patiently against it" (1 Corinthians 10:13). Perhaps right now the devil is bringing such pressure on you through temptation that you think you will either explode or collapse. Take heart. Look to Christ for help. He will help you stand firm.

LYING

Sir Thomas Browne found out three centuries ago, "The devil played at chess with me, and yielding a pawn thought to gain a queen of me, taking advantage of my honest endeavours." The devil is a master at telling half-truths and leading victims up the garden path. He capitalizes on every opportunity, not caring about what he is doing to us.

This is what happened in the Garden of Eden when Satan "beguiled Eve through his subtilty" (2 Corinthians 11:3, KJV). Whenever the devil can use innuendo, implication, or other means to achieve his ends, he will. As Thomas Carlyle put it a century ago: "Sarcasm I now see to be, in general, the language of the devil." Perhaps it gives him a bit more fiendish glee than when he reaches his sinister goals by outright lies.

It is astonishing that after a century of the "scientific method," which is supposed to have brought society to "truth," the West has turned its back on truth. A *Time* essayist affirmed that in the Western world today, " 'reason' and 'logic' have, in fact, become dirty words... The rational is presumed to be shallow and unconscious—the irrational to be where it's at ... truth is an unspeakable madness." Whoever is behind such thinking? It is the devil, the deceiver.

Jesus turned on the Pharisees one day and told them bluntly that their "father the devil" was "a hater of truth—there is not an iota of truth in him. When he lies, it is perfectly normal; for he is the father of liars. And so when I tell you the truth, you just naturally don't believe it" (John 8:44, 45). From the neutron to the undiscovered star, God as Creator founded and sustains a rational universe on the principle of truth. Subtract truth from God's creation and everything disintegrates into atomized chaos.

Christ the Creator is a constructionist and sustainer; the devil is a destructionist. His whole system is built on lies; so it is not surprising that his agents lie whenever untruth serves their purpose. Israel listened to servants of Satan despite God's warning: "Do not listen to your false prophets, fortune-tellers, dreamers, mediums and magicians who say the king of Babylon will not enslave you. For they are all liars" (Jeremiah 27:9, 10). God's message to the Ammonites was: "Your magicians and false prophets have told you lies of safety and success—that your gods will save you from the king of Babylon. Thus they have caused your death along with all the other wicked" (Ezekiel 21:29).

You can mark it down. The devil always makes his followers liars. An example is the "native genius," Carlos Castaneda, who received his Ph.D. from U.C.L.A. His books, which are based on sorcery, are making him a millionaire, according to the *Time* cover story on his life and works. The *Time* story describes him as a constant liar, giving as an example the observation of his editor at Simon and Schuster, Michael Kovda. "Carlos will call you from a phone booth," says Kovda, "and say he is in Los Angeles. Then the operator will cut in for more change, and it turns out to be Yuma (Arizona)." "Carlos' basic explanation of his lying generally," notes *Time,* is his "sorcery."

An American founding father pointed out that a lie never serves a useful purpose. Lies are the bane of the

church, the plague of politics, the cancer of society,
and the ruination of the individual. Paul informed
Timothy that in the last times, some in the church will
turn away from Christ and become eager followers of
"teachers with devil-inspired ideas. These teachers
will tell lies with straight faces and do it so often that
their consciences won't even bother them" (1 Timothy
4:1, 2).

"O! While you live," wrote Shakespeare, "tell
truth, and shame the devil!"

LUST

There is today, as Malcolm Muggeridge puts it, a
"mania for sexual excitement that has become more
and more tinged with sadism and cruelty." Lust is one
of Satan's most insidious attack tactics—expressed
in various forms of immorality: fornication, adultery,
homosexuality or lesbianism, and mental immorality.

It seems that each year we move closer to Sodom. Sex
is almost deified. In *Love and Will,* psychoanalyst
Rollo May deals with "the demons of our civilization."
He contrasts our time with a hundred years ago when
people desperately "sought to have love without
falling into sex; the modern person seeks to have sex
without falling into love."

Certainly a film like *Last Tango in Paris,* which shows
a sadomasochistic relationship between two total
strangers who engage in animalistic fornication, is an
example of lust and the degradation of sex. No
pretense of love is made. The male makes the female
submit to unprintable personal indignities as a sign of
her enslavement to him, including swearing
disallegiance to her church.

Newspaper pundit John Donnelly wrote, "I am not
a prude, nor do I have any real moral hangups about

THE DEVIL

people doing their thing." Yet he cannot think that the way "The Happy Hooker" is virtually deified and mobbed for her autograph would have been tolerated "by a community at large even ten years ago." It is, he says, a commentary on our times. Our former vices have become our present gods.

A Miss Universe was asked whether she believed in premarital sex. Without hesitation she replied, "You wouldn't buy a new frock without trying it on, would you?"

The lack of clothing can indicate the devil's influence. When Jesus arrived "in the Gerasene country ... a man from the city of Gadara came to meet him, a man who had been demon-possessed for a long time. Homeless and naked..." (Luke 8:26, 27). Satan's agents caused him to wear nothing; only when Jesus cast out the demons was he found "clothed" (8:35).

When Christian missionaries went to Africa, they often found the people naked or nearly so. When Africans became Christians, they almost invariably procured and wore clothes. Here in North America, as the drift toward paganism continues, so does the trend toward scantier attire. In an African country, a Peace Corps recruit was asked to leave because she was appearing in public very nearly in the nude. Christianity had influenced the culture of that country, which had risen from total paganism and the people wearing little. The Christian prime minister asked that the American girl either dress properly or leave the country.

History repeats itself. It seems we are like ancient Israel. God said of his people, "They do a big business as prostitutes ... they have deserted me and turned to other gods. Wine, women, and song have robbed my people of their brains.... They have played the harlot, serving other gods, deserting me" (Hosea 4:10,

126

11, 12). Addressing them directly, God warned, "Your deeds won't let you come to God again, for the spirit of adultery is deep within you, and you cannot know the Lord" (5:4).

There seems to be a strong link between adultery and the domination of the devil in people's lives. The breaking of the seventh commandment does something to harden the heart which nearly no other sin does. You can be sure there will be no turning from the immorality which is sweeping through and nearly swallowing up our society until and unless we turn back to God in repentance and faith.

A university head recently visited Red China, and on his return was asked what impressed him most. He replied that it was the fact that in China today there seems to be virtually no premarital sex, no extramarital sex, and no homosexuality. The reason, he said, was that the Chinese can do nothing without being watched. We in North America need to realize that we are being watched—watched by an all-seeing God—and that one day we will have to answer to him for our lives.

DRUNKENNESS

Closely akin to the devil and his incitement to sexual uncleanness is the sin of drunkenness. Today drink is the third greatest killer in North America. On roads in the United States alone, 35,000 people were killed in 1974 as a direct result of drunken driving.

Intoxication is not in itself demon possession. But as drugs open up the human psyche to the incoming of demons, so alcohol empties a person of the full possession of his faculties. And it is a short step indeed for the liquid spirits to make way for evil spirits. Peter reminded his readers, "You have had enough in the past of the evil things the godless enjoy—sex sin, lust, getting drunk, wild parties, drinking bouts, and the worship of idols" (1 Peter 4:3). Paul wrote to the Galatians that "idolatry, spiritism (that is, encouraging the activity of demons), hatred and fighting ... envy, murder, drunkenness, wild parties, and all that sort of thing" constituted a life-style which compelled him to repeat "that anyone living that sort of life will not inherit the kingdom of God" (5:20, 21).

In the United States are are ten million alcoholics, in Canada one million. The Apostle Paul pointed to the answer: "and be not drunk with wine, wherein is excess; but be filled with the Spirit" (Ephesians 5:18, KJV). The fullness of the Holy Spirit is the only real antidote for alcoholism.

VIOLENCE AND MURDER

The devil has been behind every murder since the death of Abel (Genesis 4:8). Paul wrote to the Romans, "When Adam sinned, sin entered the entire human race. His sin spread death throughout all the world...." (5:12). Satan has the power of death (Hebrews 2:14).

Studies reveal that the number of murders in North America has doubled in the last twenty years. A gruesome murder in England occupied the newspaper headlines throughout the country for several days. When the judge asked the accused why he had done such a heinous thing, the murderer replied, "There was someone in me who made me do it." The disciples of Charles Manson openly confessed that the devil in them incited them to kill. Arthur Bremer shot George Wallace, and in doing so probably altered the complexion of that 1972 presidential election campaign more than any other single event. He told a *Time* reporter that he would have shot either George McGovern or the president himself if he had had the chance—a compulsion inside him demanded that he kill somebody. He said, "That's how far gone I am."

A twenty-two-year-old girl in Miami killed a sixty-two-year-old man by stabbing him forty-six times. After she was sentenced to seven years for manslaughter, she smiled, said a prayer to Satan, and thanked the devil for the light sentence, adding that she enjoyed the killing.

A guest on *The Johnny Carson Show* declared that he believed Adolf Hitler was demon-possessed. That may have been true. In *The Mind of Adolf Hitler,* eminent psychiatrist Walter Langer claimed that Eva Braun, Hitler's mistress, was a witch—perhaps demon possessed.

We shudder at these things, but is not our entire society becoming permeated with evil? According to *The Chicago Tribune,* by the time the average adolescent has finished high school, he has spent 11,000 hours in the classroom and 15,000 hours watching television. According to Richard Wiley, chairman of the Federal Communications Commission, by the time a child is thirteen, he or she has witnessed on TV an average of 13,000 killings.

In the last year, violent crime increased 13 percent in the United States. During the last decade, violent crimes committed by teenage girls have increased by 276 percent. That is not exactly women's liberation. It is women's bondage. In New York City, murders increased a staggering 26 percent in one year. In London in the same year, rape shot up 50 percent, and crimes of violence 10 percent.

Murder: it's a frightening word. Yet the Bible teaches that "anyone who hates his Christian brother is really a murderer at heart; and you know

that no one wanting to murder has eternal life within"
(1 John 3:15). That is a strong indictment, but it is the
Word of God. As God is love, so the devil is hate. If you
hate a Christian or Christians, you are serving Satan.
Ethel Waters once said, "Hate is so cancerous. When
you let your temper get the best of you, who has the
headaches and high blood pressure? You. That's why
I laugh so much now. I'm not going to let the devil best
me."

MATERIALISM

How dear money and things can be!

The Apostle Paul adopted the right attitude toward
materialism when he exhorted that believers should
"use this world, as not abusing it" (1 Corinthians
7:31, KJV). On the other hand, he warned that "the
love of money is the first step toward all kinds of sin.
Some people have even turned away from God
because of their love for it, and as a result have pierced
themselves through with many sorrows" (1 Timothy
6:10).

The desire for gain had a great deal to do with the
fall of Satan. God indicted him with these words: "You
defiled your holiness with lust for gain" (Ezekiel 28:18).
Therefore it is to be expected that he would inflame his
servants with this mania. "The heads thereof judge for
reward, and the priests thereof teach for hire, and the
prophets thereof divine for money" (Micah 3:11,
KJV).

Satan sought to destroy people in the early church
through the love of money. Ananias and Sapphira let
Satan fill their hearts with a desire for wealth, and this
led to their sin and sudden deaths (Acts 5:1-10).
Simon, a former sorcerer, noted that when Peter

and John laid their hands on believers, these
believers received the Holy Spirit. Simon "offered
money to buy this power. 'Let me have this power too,'
he exclaimed, 'so that when I lay my hands on people,
they will receive the Holy Spirit!' But Peter replied,
'Your money perish with you for thinking God's gift
can be bought! You can have no part in this, for
your heart is not right before God' " (8:9-19).

Another indication of Satan's preoccupation with
gain is recorded in Acts 16. Luke described what
happened: "One day as we were going down to the
place of prayer beside the river, we met a
demon-possessed slave girl who was a fortune-teller,
and earned much money for her masters. She
followed along behind us shouting, 'These men are
servants of God and they have come to tell you how to
have your sins forgiven.' This went on day after day until
Paul, in great distress, turned and spoke to the demon
within her. 'I command you in the name of Jesus Christ
to come out of her,' he said. And instantly it left her.
Her masters' hopes of wealth were now shattered;
they grabbed Paul and Silas and dragged them before
the judges at the marketplace. 'These Jews are
corrupting our city' " (vv. 16-21). What an ironic
distortion of the truth!

Paul and Silas were thrown into jail, and around
midnight the Lord sent a "great earthquake; the prison
was shaken to its foundations, all the doors flew
open—and the chains of every prisoner fell off!" The
hysterical jailer asked his Spirit-imbued prisoners, "Sirs,
what must I do to be saved?" Paul and Silas replied,
"Believe on the Lord Jesus and you will be saved, and
your entire household" (vv. 22-31).

Satan had overstepped himself by exploiting a girl so
that her evil masters could fill up their coffers with
money. But God in his grace delivered her.

HYPOCRISY

If the love of money and the willingness to lie were a part of Satan's tactics which trapped and cut down Ananias and Sapphira, hypocrisy was another diabolical tactic evidenced in that tragic episode. One of Satan's most successful exhibits has always been the person who professes good but turns around and does evil. Shapespeare wrote about it in *Richard III:* "And thus I clothe my naked villany with odd old ends stol'n forth of holy writ, and seem a saint when most I play the devil." And in *Hamlet:* "With devotion's visage and pious action we do sugar over the devil himself."

If we are indeed in the last times, we can expect a great deal of hypocrisy. Paul predicted that "in the latter times some shall depart from the faith, giving heed to seducing spirits, and doctrines of devils; speaking lies in hypocrisy" (1 Timothy 4:1, 2, KJV). In the letter to the church of Smyrna, John wrote that some would oppose believers while claiming to be "the children of God—but they aren't, for they support the cause of Satan" (Revelation 2:9).

It is significant that the words *hypocrisy, hypocrite,* and *hypocritical* appear twenty-three times in the statements of Jesus, eight times in the Book of Job, and seven times elsewhere in the Bible.

Hypocrites are a joyless people. "The hypocrite's hope shall perish" (Job 8:13, KJV). "The congregation of hypocrites shall be desolate" (15:34, KJV). "The joy of the hypocrite [is] but for a moment" (20:5, KJV). "For what is the hope of the hypocrite, though he hath gained, when God taketh away his soul?" (27:8, KJV). "The hypocrites in the heart heap up wrath" (36:13, KJV).

Jesus warned that we should be careful not to seek recognition for good deeds (Matthew 6:1-3), pray as the hypocrites pray (6:5), fast as hypocrites fast (6:16),

or criticize our brethren while we ourselves may have
larger faults (7:1-5).

James said that the wisdom which is from above,
that is, which is God-given, is "without hypocrisy"
(3:17, KJV). We can infer that "wisdom" which is from
beneath, that is, from Satan, is full of hypocrisy.

FALSE PROPHETS

The ancient prophet Jeremiah said, "The Lord of
Hosts, the God of Israel, says: 'Don't let the false
prophets and mediums who are there among you fool
you. Don't listen to the dreams that they invent" (29:8).

The church has always been plagued with people who
claimed they received revelation from God in dreams
or visions. True, there are times when God reveals his
will through extraordinary manifestations of his Spirit.
And sometimes he makes known his will through
dreams. The Bible plainly states that in the last days
when he pours out his Spirit, "your old men will dream
dreams, and your young men see visions" (Joel 2:28).
But because the devil is such an ingenious inventor
and counterfeiter, it is most important that we "try the
spirits whether they are of God" (1 John 4:1, KJV).

The prophet Zechariah urged, "Ask the Lord ...
and he will answer... How foolish to ask the idols for
anything like that! Fortune-tellers' predictions are all a
bunch of silly lies; what comfort is there in promises that
don't come true? Judah and Israel have been led astray
and wander like lost sheep.... My anger burns against
your 'shepherds'—your leaders—and I will punish
them—these goats" (10:1-3).

Perhaps the area of truth Satan likes to attack most
is Bible prophecy. People under his influence will pose
as prophets with an alleged sixth sense. They will set
exact dates for the second advent or identify some

specially wicked ruler as the Antichrist, despite the fact that these practices are clearly forbidden in the New Testament (Matthew 24:36; 2 Thessalonians 2:3). The result can be untold grief for those who were fooled by the story, and another occasion for the enemies of Jesus Christ to heap ridicule on the church.

God deplores self-appointed inventors of "truth" who claim they have received a special revelation from the Lord, when in fact they have got a message from the devil or are simply taking off on an ego trip. With this in mind, Paul urged the Corinthians to cast down "imaginations, and every high thing that exalteth itself against the knowledge of God, and [bring] into captivity every thought to the obedience of Christ" (2 Corinthians 10:5, KJV).

One of the best illustrations of Satan getting people to abandon the ship of truth for sailboats of fantasy can be seen in Malcolm Muggeridge's *Esquire* review of Elemire Zolla's *The Eclipse of the Intellectuals*. Muggeridge characterized the book as "an illuminating and noble work which is a searching analysis of the contemporary mass man." Muggeridge quoted Zolla: "The deadly boredom of modern life demands ever new stimulants, and only this attitude of conscious duplicity, which extracts the required excitants from evil—that is, from the divorce from nature—enables one to confront it. Hence, the exaltation of evil, of the deformed, sterile, and artificial, the pleasure taken in decadence."

DEPRESSION

King Saul fought the blues with music provided by the harpist David. "Whenever the tormenting spirit troubled Saul, David would play the harp and Saul would feel better!" But eventually the "tormenting spirit overwhelmed Saul, and he began to rave like a madman" (1 Samuel 16:23; 18:10). Music was not the answer. It treated symptoms rather than causes.

Perhaps the reason why young people today seem to need so much music just in order to exist is because the devil is making an all-out attack on them by filling them with depression! The suicide rate, the drug scene, the sexual exploits, the dropouts from school, the cop-outs from society, some of the insanity and the chronic restlessness from which they suffer seem to be evidences of a continual battle to ward off depression.

Bishop Fulton Sheen remarked in 1975 that the suicide rate among youth under eighteen years old had doubled in the last two years. Psychiatrist Sol Levine puts this down to escalating alienation and spiritual despair. This may be why Brigitte Bardot has become bitter, hates humanity, rejects children, and suffers such melancholy that she has little interest in life. Dr. Fawcett, a *Chicago Tribune* columnist, says that many people today are on the verge of taking their own lives. He adds that often a person has no idea how to cope with depression. When it happens to him, he "saves" himself from it by attempting suicide. A depressed person needs to be told he has a biological illness that can be treated. The trouble is, depressed people don't feel ill, they feel like lousy people.

Psychologist Erich Fromm has said that when a person "cannot take a genuine interest in life, his boredom will force him to seek it in the perverted way of destruction and violence." Some Christian psychiatrists believe that many mental and emotional problems and illnesses result from oppression by Satan. Some of these problems are schizophrenia, neurosis, psychosis, psychoneurosis, masochism, melancholia, homosexuality, lesbianism, hallucinations, delirium

tremens, epilepsy, complexes, addictive habits,
delusions, and sudden compulsions.

The Apostle Paul felt the incessant blows of the
devil on his life, but he refused to yield to Satan's
efforts. He wrote to the Corinthians, "We are pressed on
every side by troubles, but not crushed and broken.
We are perplexed because we don't know why things
happen as they do, but we don't give up and quit. We
are hunted down, but God never abandons us. We
get knocked down, but we get up again and keep
going. These bodies of ours are constantly facing death
just as Jesus did; so it is clear to all that it is only the
living Christ within [who keeps us safe]"
(2 Corinthians 4:8-10).

WORLDLINESS
Worldliness is not the violation of certain traditional
taboos, but rather it is having the same *attitude* toward
things as does the world. Conformity to the world's
attitudes and values has always been a tactic of the devil.

The Apostle Paul exhorted his fellow believers,
"Don't be teamed with those who do not love the
Lord, for what do the people of God have in
common with the people of sin? How can light live
with darkness? And what harmony can there be
between Christ and the devil? How can a Christian be a
partner with one who doesn't believe? And what union
can there be between God's temple and idols? For you
are God's temple, the home of the living God, and God
has said of you, 'I will live in them and walk among
them, and I will be their God and they shall be my
people.' That is why the Lord has said, 'Leave them;
separate yourself from them; don't touch their filthy
things, and I will welcome you, and be a Father to
you, and you will be my sons and daughters' "

(2 Corinthians 6:14-18). He also wrote to the
Romans, "Don't copy the behavior and customs of
this world, but be a new and different person with a
fresh newness in all you do and think" (12:2).

When you try to harmonize Christ and the devil, all
you get is blaring discord. That is precisely what Satan
tries to engender in your life. He wants to mingle the
pure and the impure—the result is more impurity.

The Apostle John said, "Stop loving this evil
world and all that it offers you, for when you love
these things you show that you do not really love God;
for all these worldly things, these evil desires—the craze
for sex, the ambition to buy everything that appeals to
you, and the pride that comes from wealth and
importance—these are not from God. They are from
this evil world itself. And this world is fading away
and these evil, forbidden things will go with it, but
whoever keeps doing the will of God will live forever"
(1 John 2:15-17). When we refuse to copy the world, we
can expect trouble. "We are not to be like Cain, who
belonged to Satan and killed his brother. Why did he kill
him? Because Cain had been doing wrong and he knew
very well that his brother's life was better than his.
So don't be surprised, dear friends, if the world hates
you" (3:12-13).

1 John 2:15-17 was the life passage of Dwight L.
Moody, the great evangelist of the last century. For
many years he had done battle with the devil. Satan's
image kept coming through to him in the form of
worldliness. Then one day, on the streets of New York,
just after his possessions had gone up in the
great Chicago fire of 1871, he surrendered all his
worldly assets and ambitions to Jesus Christ. During the
next twenty-five years Moody traveled throughout this
continent and the British Isles, turning hundreds of
thousands of people to faith in Christ as Savior and Lord.

THE DEVIL

JEALOUSY
The devil is never more gratified than when he can use a festering, poisoning sin of the spirit.

"Jealousy," wrote James, is "... not God's kind of wisdom." It is "inspired by the devil" (3:15). Jealousy has toppled thrones, split churches, broken marriages, and stacked up the remains of lives which once cruised down the freeway of holiness and prosperity.

When Peter arrived at Samaria and was approached by Simon the former sorcerer, he commanded Simon to repent. Repent of what? "I can see that there is jealousy and sin," noted Peter, "in your heart" (Acts 8:23).

The wise Solomon said, "Jealousy is more dangerous and cruel than anger" (Proverbs 27:4). The reason why jealousy is so devastating is because it is not something you go to bed with, wake up, and find it gone. It lingers; it is often chronic. It is an acid which eats away at the tissue and fiber of a man's character until he is destroyed.

ANGER
Anger can be a destructive, incendiary force which opens a person up to the devil's destruction. Neither jealousy nor anger in itself is wrong. God, according to the Scriptures, often feels both. His love is a jealous love; he is angry with the wicked. But what is wrong is an anger which is nursed along into hate, or allowed to burn out of control. Paul wrote to the Ephesians, "If you are angry, don't sin by nursing your grudge. Don't let the sun go down with you still angry—get over it quickly; for when you are angry you give a mighty foothold to the devil" (Ephesians 4:26, 27).

Moses was once angry at the wandering Israelites because of their sin, unbelief, and disobedience to God. The fact that Moses was angry at Israel was not sin. But when he was angry, he failed to control his temper. That was his undoing. He struck the rock to provide water for Israel when God had told him to only speak to it. But the people's complaining had angered Moses, and his inability to control his temper cost him the privilege of entering the Promised Land (Numbers 20:7-12).

From ancient times, Satan has been a wholesaler of anger. Solomon, the revelator of ancient wisdom, urged, "Keep away from angry, short-tempered men, lest you learn to be like them and endanger your soul" (Proverbs 22:24, 25). He also reckoned that it was "better to dwell in the wilderness, than with a contentious and angry woman" (21:19, KJV). "A hot-tempered man starts fights and gets into all kinds of trouble" (29:22).

All of us can live better lives if we can be free of that kind of conduct. Take your temper to the Lord, and he will replace it with the fruit of his Spirit, "gentleness and self-control" (Galatians 5:23).

SELFISHNESS

Selfishness is also "inspired by the devil" (James 3:15). He seeks to fill the church with it. He sought to make Jesus think only of his own wants and needs. But Jesus told his disciples, "Anyone who wants to follow me must put aside his own desires and conveniences and carry his cross with him every day and *keep close to me*. Whoever loses his life for my sake will save it, but whoever insists on keeping his life will lose it" (Luke 9:23, 24).

"Don't be selfish," wrote Paul to the Philippians. "Your attitude should be the kind that was shown us by Jesus Christ, who, though he was God, did not demand and cling to his rights as God, but laid aside his mighty power and glory, taking the disguise of a slave and becoming like men" (Philippians 2:3, 5, 6).

It would be impossible to enumerate the areas where Satan is using his weapon of selfishness. One example, however, is marriage. In marriage, according to psychiatrist Victor Frankl, much of the sexual neurosis today comes because "rather than thinking of self-giving and loving encounter, there is a turning in on self with resultant frustration." The old problem of self ruins marriages, as well as individuals, churches, institutions, and organizations. Psychoanalyst Rollo May sees self-interest in sex as a modern curse. "Our new found sexual freedom has robbed us of real love and liberty, resulting in a new puritanism worse than the old, based on cool noninvolvement and mythical self-sufficiency."

FALSE INTELLECTUALISM

One of Satan's peculiar and surprising attack tactics is a perverted intellectual sophistication, at which he is a master. Pope Paul calls it "utopian logic." Satan is a sophisticate, a real intellectual snob. If the devil can muddy the waters and get men to dive to admirable depths of thought from which they come up with profound-sounding arguments—arguments which shake your belief in God, your faith in the integrity of his character, or your adherence to the rationality of his acts—Satan has made a substantial gain.

Paul said he was "not ignorant of his [Satan's] devices" (2 Corinthians 2:11, KJV). We too often overlook intellectualism in our passionate zeal for education. Let us never forget, however, that Satan pulled the rug out from under us by tempting Eve to eat the fruit "of the tree of the knowledge of good and evil" (Genesis 2:17, KJV). Was knowledge wrong? Of course not. In Christ, Paul told the Colossians, "lie hidden all the mighty, untapped treasures of wisdom and knowledge" (Colossians 2:3). The problem was that man was not capable of coping with the knowledge of good and evil. His moral defense mechanisms were too fragile. It was like giving a blowtorch to a three-year-old in a dynamite factory. Man failed to recognize his limitations and to ask God for needed strength.

The Duke of Wellington, who defeated Napoleon at Waterloo and later became a great prime minister of England, contended for the education of the masses, but he cautioned, "Educate men without religion and you make them but clever devils." We see the truth of that in General Omar Bradley's warning that modern man is not likely to survive, since we have too many men in our world who are at once thermonuclear giants and moral morons.

All too easily, Paul wrote to the Corinthians, men can be "outsmarted by Satan" (2 Corinthians 2:11). He warned the Colossians, "Don't let others spoil your faith and joy with their philosophies, their wrong and shallow answers built on men's thoughts and ideas, instead of on what Christ has said" (2:8). To his son in the faith, he wrote, "Oh, Timothy ... keep out of foolish arguments with those who boast of their 'knowledge' and thus prove their lack of it" (1 Timothy 6:20).

For more than a century the world has been reeling from the impact of the writings of Karl Marx, Charles Darwin, and Sigmund Freud. The impressive use of statistics, facts, theories, human behavior patterns, and historic trends are all used in an effort to turn man to humanism. It is a clever tactic of Satan. *Time* magazine reported the "story of how a European rationalist was initiated into the practice of Indian sorcery ... over a span of ten years," during which this "academic" achieved a "separate reality," presenting his case not "as fiction but as unembellished documentary

fact." This incredible trend of selling out intellectually
to the devil will increase. This kind of "learning,"
notes *Time*, "is a common theme in the favorite reading
of young Americans today," to the extent that
"more Americans than ever before are disposed to
consider 'no rational' approaches to reality."

What are Christians to do? The defense our Lord
calls for is that we "hold tightly to what you have
until I come" (Revelation 2:24). We are to content
ourselves with knowing and obeying what God has
already revealed. The rest we can learn about when we
are forever with Christ. Paul clearly said we cannot
know or understand everything fully. "We can see and
understand only a little about God now, as if we
were peering at his reflection in a poor mirror; but
someday we are going to see him in his completeness,
face to face. Now all that I know is hazy and blurred, but
then I will see everything clearly" (1 Corinthians 13:12).

Was Judas the only man ever to betray the Son of
God? No. When each person comes to his personal
crossroads, he consigns Jesus Christ either to the
cross in his life or to the throne of his life as King.

By refusing Jesus Christ as your Savior and Lord, you
betray him all over again. In your failure to "repent ...
you have nailed the Son of God to the cross again by
rejecting him, holding him up to mocking and to public
shame" (Hebrews 6:6).

Don't do it any longer. If you have any doubt about
whether or not you are a Christian, set this book down
this minute, bow your head, and pray in sincere faith,
"Jesus Christ, Son of Almighty God, I absolutely
refuse to allow Satan any longer to dupe me into
betraying you. I ask you to come into my heart and
life, to be my Savior and Lord, now and forever-
more. Thank you, Lord Jesus!"

CHAPTER NINE

Dare to Confront the Devil

Most people are citizens of the devil's kingdom, even if they don't know it. Jesus said plainly that "the highway to hell is broad, and its gate is wide enough for all the multitudes who choose its easy way. But the Gateway to Life is small, and the road is narrow, and only a few ever find it. Beware of false teachers who come disguised as harmless sheep, but are wolves and will tear you apart" (Matthew 7:13-15). The point is that the devil dispatches his forces to hoodwink the majority of people into following him.

This tragic situation can be turned around—if it is confronted honestly. Unless you have the assurance of the Word of God and the witness of the Holy Spirit that you are a child of God, you are a child of the devil. That is not very flattering, but God said it (John 8:44; Romans 8:9). You may be a church member, but that does not mean you are a child of God. It was of charter members of the first churches that Paul demanded, "Check up on yourselves. Are you really Christians? Do you pass the test? Do you feel Christ's presence and power more and more within you? Or are you just pretending to be Christians when actually you aren't at all?" (2 Corinthians 13:5). Let us keep in mind that to very religious people Jesus said, "You are the children of your father the devil and you love to do the evil things he does" (John 8:44).

This leads us to conclude that in determining whose child you are, you must see whether your sympathies lean toward what the devil favors or what Christ favors. "If you keep on sinning, it shows that you belong to Satan" (1 John 3:8), wrote the Apostle John. Getting even more specific, he said, "So now we can tell who is a child of God and who belongs to Satan. Whoever is living a life of sin and doesn't love his brother shows that he is not in God's family" (3:10).

What characterizes the person who may pass as a Christian but who has never really been born again? Paul dealt with this question in his first letter to the Corinthians when he said, "Don't fool yourselves. Those who live immoral lives, who are idol worshipers, adulterers or homosexuals—will have no share in his [Christ's] kingdom. Neither will thieves or greedy people, drunkards, slanderers, or robbers" (6:9-10). Paul went on to make it clear that he was not referring to those who once were these kinds of people. He meant that those who presently practiced these sins could not under any circumstances think of themselves as Christians. He said, "There was a time when some of you were just like that but now your sins are washed away, and you are set apart for God, and he has accepted you because of what the Lord Jesus Christ and the Spirit of our God have done for you" (6:11).

The devil would like very much to keep you thinking
that as long as you pretend to be a Christian, you are
one. But this no more makes you a Christian than
moving to the United States makes a European an
American. To be an American you either have to be
born an American or you have to take out citizenship
papers and become an American. To be a Christian, you
have to give up citizenship in the kingdom of Satan and
become a naturalized citizen of the kingdom of God by
being adopted into the family of God. Paul reminded
the Colossians how God "has made us fit to share
all the wonderful things that belong to those who live
in the kingdom of light. For he has rescued us out of the
darkness and gloom of Satan's kingdom and brought us
into the kingdom of his dear Son, who bought our
freedom with his blood and forgave us all our sins"
(1:12-14). Regardless of the nature, number, and
frequency of your sins, when you opt to be "born
again" into God's family, you are released from
Satan's hold, and Jesus Christ transplants you from the
kingdom of Satan into his own kingdom.

Face the fact—to escape the devil, you must be born
again.

Jesus said, "You must be born again" (John 3:7).
He did not say that this would be a good idea to
consider. No, Jesus said, even to no less a man than
Nicodemus, a member of a select religious body, "You
must be born again."

Hence, to confront the devil, you must admit your
need and turn to Christ for help. You can't get into the
kingdom of God without being born again, and you
can't get out of the kingdom of Satan without being
born again. You cannot take up citizenship in one
country in this world without renouncing your
citizenship in another.

How are you "born again?" By receiving by faith the

good news that Christ died for your sins, that he gave his lifeblood on the cross that he might cleanse you of your sin, and that he can give you the gift of eternal life. If you receive Christ into your life as your personal Savior and eternal Lord, you have the authoritative promise of his Word that you are born again. "Seeing ye have purified your souls in obeying the truth through the Spirit," wrote Peter, you can know that you have been "born again, not of corruptible seed, but of incorruptible, by the word of God, which liveth and abideth for ever" (1 Peter 1:22, 23, KJV). That experience, and that experience alone, gets you out of the kingdom of Satan into the kingdom of God.

Martin Luther once said, "Once upon a time the devil came to me and said, 'Martin, you are a great sinner, and you will be damned!' 'Stop! Stop' said I. 'One thing at a time. I am a sinner, it is true, though you have no right to tell me of it. I confess it. What next?' 'Therefore you will be damned.' 'That is not good reasoning. It is true I am a great sinner, but it is written, "Christ Jesus came into the world to save sinners, of whom I am chief," therefore I shall be saved. Now go your way.' " Martin Luther could say, like Paul, "Who is he that condemneth? It is Christ that died, yea rather, that is risen again!" (Romans 8:34, KJV).

Victorious confrontation with the devil is based on the realization that on your own you are no match for him. In Christ, however, you are united to the One to whom Satan is subject. Paul exulted in the fact that God raised Christ "to the heights of heaven and gave him a name which is above every other name, that at the name of Jesus, every knee shall bow in heaven and on earth and under the earth [including Satan and his evil legions], and every tongue shall confess that Jesus Christ is Lord, to the glory of God the Father" (Philippians 2:9-11). Peter affirmed, "And now Christ is in heaven, sitting in the place of honor next to God the Father, with all the angels and powers of heaven bowing before him and obeying him" (1 Peter 3:22). And he is praying for you there.

Convinced beyond doubt of this fact, Paul, while a prisoner in an ugly jail, could bask in the sunshine of the glorious promise that "overwhelming victory is ours through Christ who loved us enough to die for us. For I am convinced that nothing can ever separate us from his love. Death can't, and life can't. The angels won't, and all the powers of hell itself cannot keep God's love away. Our fears for today, our worries about tomorrow, or where we are—high above the sky, or in the deepest ocean—nothing will ever be able to separate us from the love of God demonstrated by our Lord Jesus Christ when he died for us" (Romans 8:38).

Bold confrontation with Satan and his demons is possible because Jesus Christ is far above the jurisdiction of Satan. Whenever you level with the devil, or however adverse your circumstances, cling tenaciously to this fact. The Russian Christians greet each other when they meet, "Jesus Christ is risen," and they reply, "Yes, he is risen indeed!" I wish that were our hello and good-bye here in North America.

Because Christ is risen, we can lay claim to triumph before we ever enter a contest with Satan and his demons. Jesus gave the reason: "I am the Good Shepherd and know my own sheep, and they know me, just as my Father knows me and I know the Father; and I lay down my life for the sheep" (John 10:14). So Jesus is ever caring for us, and without his care we could never win over sin or the devil. Another one of the great promises of the Word of God in this regard is Hebrews 7:24, 25, where we are assured that

THE DEVIL

"Jesus lives forever and continues to be a Priest so that no one else is needed. He is able to save completely all who come to God through him. Since he will live forever, he will always be there to remind God that he has paid for their sins with his blood."

Satan and his demons know full well that their only challenge to Christ, besides controlling their own followers, is to try and win battles over Christians by bluff or default. But we can be assured, as was Hudson Taylor, founder of the China Inland Mission, that "Satan the hinderer may build a barrier about us, but he can never roof us in." An elderly saint once said, "The devil can put me in a big dark bottle, but thank God he can never shove in the cork!"

An interesting instance of the believer's constant recourse to Christ by faith is found in Acts 19, where we read of "a team of itinerant Jews [not Christians] who were traveling from town to town casting out demons." Having witnessed the transformations which had been going on under Paul's ministry in the Turkish province of Asia, these itinerants decided "to experiment by using the name of the Lord Jesus. The incantation they decided on was this: 'I adjure you by Jesus, whom Paul preaches, to come out!' Seven sons of Sceva, a Jewish priest, were doing this. But when they tried it on a man possessed by a demon, the demon replied, 'I know Jesus and I know Paul, but who are you?' And he leaped on two of them and beat them up, so that they fled out of his house naked and badly injured. The story of what happened spread quickly all through Ephesus, to Jews and Greeks alike; and a solemn fear descended on the city, and the name of the Lord Jesus was greatly honored" (vv. 13-17).

Many relevant lessons can be learned from this account, but particularly note two. One is that if you

don't belong to Jesus Christ and if you start playing the
Satan game, demons can overtake you and do
through you whatever Satan masterminds. Note also
that the demons were immediately cognizant of who
Jesus was and who Paul the Christian was. When you
become a Christian, Satan and all his agents become
aware of who you are and what you are about.

The devil begins to waver and turn heel when you
wield your Christ-given authority in implicit
obedience to the lordship of Jesus. The Apostle
James, exhorting believers to activate their belief into
constant obedience to Christ, emphasized, "Are there
still some among you who hold that 'only believing' is
enough? Believing in one God? Well, remember that the
demons believe this too—so strongly that they tremble
in terror! Fool! When will you ever learn that
'believing' is useless without *doing* what God wants
you to? Faith that does not result in good deeds is not
real faith" (James 2:19, 20).

So get out of the stands as a spectator of the
Christian life, and get down into the arena where the
action is. There is the confrontation. There is the
adventure. There is the conquest. But be absolutely
sure that you confront Satan and his hordes with
Jesus as your Lord. Demons bow to him. In Luke's
account we read that as our Lord went forth among the
people he encountered those who "were possessed by
demons; and the demons came out at his command,
shouting, 'You are the Son of God.' But because they
knew he was the Christ, he stopped them and told
them to be silent" (Luke 4:41). The demons obeyed
Christ; we also ought to obey him. There are too many
Christians who fit Shakespeare's words in *Othello:*
"those that will not serve God if the devil bid you."

To confront the devil victoriously, you must be fully
equipped with all of God's provision for the contest. In

his letter to the Ephesians Paul stressed, "I want to
remind you that your strength must come from the
Lord's mighty power within you. Put on all of God's
armor so that you will be able to stand safe against all
strategies and tricks of Satan.... Use every piece of
God's armor to resist the enemy whenever he attacks,
and when it is all over, you will still be standing up.
But to do this, you will need the strong belt of truth
and the breastplate of God's approval. Wear shoes
that are able to speed you on as you preach the Good
News of peace with God. In every battle you will need
faith as your shield to stop the fiery arrows aimed at
you by Satan. And you will need the helmet of salvation
and the Sword of the Spirit—which is the Word of
God. Pray all the time. Ask God for anything in line
with the Holy Spirit's wishes. Plead with him,
reminding him of your needs, and keep praying
earnestly for all Christians everywhere. Pray for me,
too.... I am in chains now for preaching this message
from God. But pray that I will keep on speaking out
boldly for him, even here in prison" (6:10, 11, 13-20).

We need to be on the offensive for Christ. We have to
realize that Christ gives us the power to beat the devil
at his own game. Remembering that the devil came to
man as a serpent, let us also remember that Jesus told
us to be "wise as serpents, and harmless as doves"
(Matthew 10:16, KJV). He told us that often "the
children of this world are in their generation wiser than
the children of light" (Luke 16:18, KJV). Rowland Hill
once remarked that he did not see any reason why the
devil should have all the good tunes, a thought echoed
by Christian pops singer Larry Norman in this
generation. Or as Coleridge put it in *The Rime of the
Ancient Mariner,* "The devil knows how to row."

We should be overwhelmed with gratitude that Paul
was prepared to put his life totally on the line for Jesus

Christ, to go forth to do battle for Christ. He was ready
to invade any stronghold of Satan which he felt might be
standing as an obstacle to the progress of the gospel.

Protected by the armor of God, we can challenge
every stronghold of the devil which confronts us. We
can level with the devil wherever we see his
cloven-hoofed footsteps. When was the last time we
picked up the Bible and let God ask us, "Why are you
trying to find out the future by consulting witches and
mediums? Don't listen to their whisperings and
mutterings. Can the living find out the future from
the dead? Why not ask your God?" (Isaiah 8:19).
Many people today treat witchcraft, necromancy, and
fortune-telling as curiosities or amusements. God never
does!

Many others take these forbidden areas very
seriously. The media tell us regularly of such
practices. A prominent prime minister has made
most of his crucial decisions on the basis of
instructions he has received from spirit mediums. Yet
we hardly raise an eyebrow. We read that a football star
marries on the basis of instructions from the Ouija
board, and we scarcely notice it.

How many of the leaders in the Western world
would think to turn for help to the followers of Jesus
Christ as Nebuchadnezzar turned to the Hebrew
children? "King Nebuchadnezzar had long talks with
each of them [young men in training], and none of them
impressed him as much as Daniel, Hananiah,
Misha-el, and Azariah. So they were put on his regular
staff of advisors. And in all matters requiring
information and balanced judgment, the king found
these young men's advice ten times better than that
of all the skilled magicians and wise astrologers in his
realm" (Daniel 1:19, 20).

Daniel was young at this time, and two generations

THE DEVIL

later he was again at it. This time an empire was
tottering on the edge of ruin. King Belshazzar had
thrown a feast for a thousand of his lords, and in the
midst of their drunkenness and lewdness, suddenly
"they saw the fingers of a man's hand writing on the
plaster of the wall opposite the lampstand. The king
himself saw the fingers as they wrote. His face
blanched with fear, and such terror gripped him that his
knees knocked together and his legs gave way beneath
him. 'Bring the magicians and astrologers!' he
screamed. 'Bring the Chaldeans! Whoever reads that
writing on the wall, and tells me what it means, will be
dressed in purple robes of royal honor' " (5:5-7).
Belshazzar was in a state of panic, but all the demon
workers proved to be completely useless. So the Queen
Mother stepped into the situation and reminded
Belshazzar of Daniel, who, she assured him,
could undoubtedly handle the situation because God
Almighty was his Lord. "He can interpret dreams,
explain riddles, and solve knotty problems" (5:12).

So Daniel was brought in. Belshazzar admitted that
his "wise men and astrologers have tried to read that
writing on the wall, and tell me what it means, but they
can't" (5:15).

Daniel told him what it meant, and history records
the catastrophe Belshazzar and his kingdom underwent
that night. It seems that many governments today are
tottering on the edge of ruin. The handwriting is
already on the wall. We need to be Daniels in our own
societies.

We also need to confront the devil in the church. He
was in the early church. In Ephesus, "many of the
believers who had been practicing black magic
confessed their deeds and brought their incantation
books and charms and burned them at a public
bonfire. (Someone estimated the value of the books

152

at $10,000)'' (Acts 19:18, 19).

Ironically, Paul used the devil to do the Lord's work of purging the church at Ephesus. Another time Paul used the devil to punish other believers. Writing to Timothy, he said, "Cling tightly to your faith in Christ and always keep your conscience clear, doing what you know is right. For some people have disobeyed their consciences and have deliberately done what they knew was wrong. It isn't surprising that soon they lost their faith in Christ after defying God like that. Hymenaeus and Alexander are two examples of this. I had to give them over to Satan to punish them until they could learn not to bring shame to the name of Christ" (1 Timothy 1:19, 20).

This was not the only time Paul referred to this recourse of the church. When a man in the Corinthian assembly was living in open immorality with his stepmother, Paul described it as "something so evil that even the heathen don't do it" (1 Corinthians 5:1). The uncompromising apostle demanded, "Cast out this man from the fellowship of the church and into Satan's hands." Why? "To punish him [footnote: for the destruction of the flesh], in the hope that his soul will be saved when our Lord Jesus Christ returns" (5:5). That man, thank God, responded to discipline and repented.

Paul's fellow apostle, Peter, exhorted, "The time has come for judgment, and it must begin first among God's own children. And if even we who are Christians must be judged, what terrible fate awaits those who have never believed in the Lord?" (1 Peter 4:17).

The greatest need in the church today is renewal and awakening—more Bible study, prayer, fasting, doing good works, witnessing. Many churches, with crying need all around, neither want to nor are able to bring people to Christ and live holy lives. This is

because they have never confronted the devil in their
midst and challenged him to withdraw. Nor have many
of them confronted a Hymenaeus, an Alexander, or a
Corinthian immoralist and removed the pollutants.

None of us is immune to a feeling of frailty or
fright over the inroads of the devil into the
institutions and social circles in which we move. Never
in history have we so much needed to use Paul's key to
the confrontation and conquest of Satan: "I don't use
human plans and methods to win my battles. I use
God's mighty weapons, not those made by men, to
knock down the devil's strongholds. These
weapons can break down every proud argument
against God and every wall that can be built to keep
men from finding him. With these weapons I can capture
rebels and bring them back to God, and change them
into men whose hearts' desire is obedience to Christ. I
will use these weapons against every rebel who
remains after I have first used them on you
yourselves, and you surrender to Christ"
(2 Corinthians 10:3-6).

Man is an undeniably religious creature. Through his
religions, he seeks to relate his daily experience to
what he intuitively senses must exist beyond the limits
of his experience. In this context the resurgence of
witchcraft and satanism is understandable. These
practices are not the pursuit of nothing, but desperate
attempts to find meaning in life. A generation which
seeks knowledge, power, and ecstasy outside the reality
of Jesus Christ exposes itself to the direct attack of
Satan. But generations are made up of individuals, and
only as we confront Satan as individuals protected
with the armor of God are we going to see an impact
on society at large. Composers Alexander Scriabin
And George Frederick Händel demonstrate the

difference between running with Satan and facing up
to Satan.

Alexander Scriabin, born on Christmas Day in 1871,
was the most controversial composer of his day. At
the age of twenty-one, he won a gold medal at the
Moscow Conservatory and later composed and
performed some of the most difficult piano pieces ever
written. His early piano etudes are exquisite miniatures,
possessing a harmony expressive of an ethereal vision
of beauty. After successful concerts throughout Europe,
he returned to Moscow in 1898 to become the
youngest professor ever to teach at the Conservatory.
At the turn of the century, he began dabbling in
Eastern mysticism. His intensely romantic
imagination flourished on intoxicating new visions of
freedom and power. In his *Divine Poem,* composed in
1903, he portrayed man's escape from the fetters of
religion and his own past, in ecstatic and triumphant
music. Though lionized by friends and admirers, his
position at the Conservatory failed to satisfy him. In
his journal he complained about the unbearable
burden of listening to other people's music all day
and being forced to write his own at night. A year later,
at the age of thirty-two, Scriabin scandalized
Moscow by deserting his wife and four children to live
openly in Switzerland with his pretty mistress,
Tatyana Schloezer.

By this time, Scriabin was possessed of a
delirious messianic vision. After four years of
immersing himself in theosophy, he had arrived at a
new and feverish vision of transforming the world
through his music. Relaxing on the shores of Lake
Geneva in 1905, he wrote in his notebook, "I am desire,
I am light ... I am the boundary, I am the summit. I am
nothing. I am God!" He startled fishermen by
preaching to them from a boat on the lake. "I am

come," he said, "to tell you the secret of life, the secret of death, the secret of heaven and hell."

Yet this mystic visionary was a frail little man plagued with intense anxieties and compulsive habits. "A sort of uneasiness, an expectation of something horrible," he wrote, "lives inside me and torments me continuously." He washed his hands compulsively, even after merely shaking hands. He slipped on gloves to give money to tradesmen in order to avoid contamination. He constantly exceeded prescribed dosages of medicines, put on an overcoat to open a window in winter, and was terrified by thunder.

Scriabin spent the next five years composing, touring Europe, and involving himself more and more in his philosophical studies and in a pursuit of new experience. His soaring symphonies seemed to come easily from his hands, but his continual expansion of the harmonic structure through dissonance and atonality confused and enraged concertgoers of his day. They failed to understand or recognize the mystical statement expressed in the music. Scriabin's *Poem of Ecstasy* depicted the "ecstasy of unfettered action." Of this symphony Scriabin wrote, "When you listen to *Ecstasy,* look straight into the eye of the sun." He discovered deities more lean and proud than Jesus Christ. "For my part," he said, "I prefer Prometheus or Satan, the prototype of revolt and individuality. Here I am my own master. I want truth, not salvation." And in his last symphony, *Prometheus, the Poem of Fire,* he described the omnipotence of the "creative will." Marked by shimmering brilliance and novelty, it proved to be his greatest symphony, supported by an elaborate light show. To Scriabin each note of the scale evoked a different color: E was like moonlight, A-sharp had the "glint of steel." Scriabin worked out the color scheme for *Prometheus* on a light machine consisting of twelve different colored bulbs, corresponding to the twelve-tone scale.

Finally he conceived of a new religion, infused with the power of all the arts. He wrote, "Art must unite with philosophy and religion in an indivisible whole to form a new gospel, which will replace the old gospel we have outlived. I cherish the dream of creating such a 'mystery.' For it, it would be necessary to build a special temple, perhaps here [in Moscow], perhaps far away in India."

The "special temple" was to be the stage for the most ambitious event ever envisioned by a famous artist. At the foot of the Himalayas, the peoples of the world would gather to attend a creative act so powerful it would cause time to end. This "mysterium," presided over by Scriabin himself, would be celebrated through a synthesis of music, dancing, poetry, colors, and perfume. The ritual would be conducted in a language of sighs and cries and exclamations. In a moment of artistic ecstasy, the human race would be transformed into another, higher and nobler. "I shall not die," Scriabin used to say, "I shall suffocate in ecstasy after the 'mysterium.' "

With apocalyptic fervor, Scriabin dedicated the last years of his life to this "ultimate work." He took up yoga breathing exercises, began the study of Sanskrit, and purchased a plot of land at the foot of the Himalayas in Darjeeling, India. He began composing a *Prefatory Action* with white-hot enthusiasm. "Animals, insects, birds, all must be there," he cried. "What happiness to tear the world apart with millions of eagles, tigers, to peck at it with kisses, to give pain and again to caress." But he had completed no more than the text and a few musical sketches when, in 1915, he developed a boil on his lip and the infection poisoned

his bloodstream. "This means the end," he
mourned as he lay dying. "But what a catastrophe."

What irony that a man born on Christmas Day should
totally reject the good news of "God with us" and openly
embrace Satan as his hero and god. Scriabin's
awareness that his decision was an act of revolt against
God and a rejection of God's gift of salvation is
remarkable. He appears to have cast himself in the
role of the Antichrist. He imitated Jesus' action in
teaching men from a boat on the lake; he even aped the
self-revelatory language of Jesus when he described
himself as desire, light, and God. He determined to
replace the gospel of life through faith in Jesus' death
and resurrection with a gospel of his own conception,
a celebration of Satan and cosmic death.

It is strange that he seemed completely unaware
that the experience of "something horrible" living
inside him and tormenting him continually was a result of
his deliberate rejection of God and his embracing of
Satan as the lord of his life. It is the supreme irony that
at the height of his powers, when his own apocalyptic
vision promised him ultimate fulfillment, his mouth
was sealed through a boil on his lip. The vision
inspired by Satan was false, the promise of ultimate
fulfillment was a lie, and the response to total devotion to
personal, radical evil was physical and spiritual death.

With Scriabin's work contrast the vision expressed
in George Frederick Händel's oratorio *Messiah*,
which in conception, scope, and intensity of
commitment rivals Scriabin's projected "mysterium."
It demanded of the composer the same white heat of
enthusiasm, and was completed in twenty-four days,
from August 22 to September 14, 1741. The oratorio
begins with a word of promise, based upon the assurance
that God has graciously moved toward his people
in order to lead them in a pageant of triumph:

Comfort ye, comfort ye my people, saith your
God; speak ye comfortably to Jerusalem; and cry
unto her, that her warfare is accomplished,
that her iniquity is pardoned. The voice of him
that crieth in the wilderness, prepare ye the
way of the Lord, make straight in the desert
a highway for our God.

The glory of the Lord is unveiled in a Son, who is
"Emmanuel, God with us," whose coming shatters the
"gross darkness" which envelops the people. The
gracious invitation is:

Come unto him, all ye that labor and are heavy
laden, and he shall give you rest. Take his
yoke upon you, and learn of him; for he is
meek and lowly of heart: and ye shall find rest
for your souls."

This is affirmed with the choral anthem:

His yoke is easy and his burden is light.

The mood changes in the second part of the oratorio
with the chorus,

Behold the Lamb of God, that taketh away
the sins of the world.

The invitation is spurned. The Son of God is despised
and rejected of men; he is an object of scorn and
ridicule and the focus of God's judgment upon the
transgression of men. The proud spirit of revolt and
individuality, so prized by Scriabin, is vividly
expressed in the bass aria:

Why do the nations so furiously rage
together? Why do the people imagine a vain
thing? The kings of the earth rise up, and the

THE DEVIL

> rulers take counsel together against the Lord,
> and against his Anointed.

This is followed by the choral chant,

> Let us break their bonds asunder, and cast
> away their yokes from us.

The arrogance and futility of this proud and lean disposition is met with scornful derision, and the triumph of God is celebrated in the "Hallelujah Chorus":

> Hallelujah! for the Lord God omnipotent
> reigneth. The kingdom of this world is become
> the kingdom of our Lord, and of his Christ;
> and he shall reign forever and ever. King of
> kings, and Lord of lords. Hallelujah!

The last movement is a vibrant expression of hope, grounded in the assurance of the resurrection, as Händel brings together Job's mighty affirmation of faith and Paul's triumphant assertion of Jesus' ressurrection.

> I know that my Redeemer liveth, and that he
> shall stand at the latter day upon the earth: And
> though worms destroy this body, yet in my flesh
> shall I see God. For now is Christ risen from
> the dead, the first-fruits of them that sleep.

Händel's final statement is a hymn of love and praise to Jesus Christ, in which all of redeemed humanity joins.

> Worthy is the Lamb that was slain, and hath
> redeemed us to God by his blood, to receive
> power, and riches, and wisdom, and strength,
> and honor, and glory, and blessing. Blessing
> and honor, glory and power, be unto him that
> sitteth upon the throne, and unto the Lamb,
> forever and ever. Amen.

Messiah is clearly a biblical statement, but it is also an intensely personal statement through which Händel expresses his own commitment. This is particularly evident in the perspective achieved through the alteration of Jesus' word of invitation, "Come unto me ... and I will give you rest," to "Come unto him ... and he will give you rest." Here Händel speaks, lending the weight of his own experience of rest through Jesus Christ to the words of his Lord.

In the music of Scriabin and Händel, we are confronted with two diametrically opposed life-styles which make the point that either man will affirm, consciously or unconsciously, the lordship of Satan and opt for cosmic death, or he will celebrate life and redemption through Jesus Christ, whose death on behalf of men and triumphant resurrection prompts the shout, "Worthy is the Lamb."

CHAPTER TEN

How to Checkmate the Devil

A famous painting had long hung in a European gallery—no one seemed to know for how long. It showed a chessboard with the devil sitting on a chair on one side, a look of gloating triumph all over his face. Across from him was a dejected, forlorn youth, defeat stamped on a still studying countenance. The title told the story: "Checkmated."

Paul Morphy, the only American chess champion of the world prior to Bobby Fischer, once toured Europe and visited that gallery. He gazed at the painting in silent reflection for a long time. Then excitedly he exclaimed, "Bring me a chessboard! There's one—only one, mind you—but there's one move whereby I can save him!"

Christ, the Lord of the universe, looked down from heaven and saw our plight. The world was checkmated by the

THE DEVIL

devil, but the Redeemer of man made the one move that
could free us from gloom in life and doom in
eternity—he died to free us from Satan's bondage.

With his staff officers around him, Napoleon
Bonaparte once spread a large map of the world on
a table before him, put his finger on a country colored
red, and said to them, "Messieurs, if it were not for that
red spot I could conquer the world." That red spot was
the British Isles.

The devil gathers his lieutenants about him, points his
index finger at Calvary, where the blood of the Son of
God was shed, and ruefully moans, "But for that
red spot, I could conquer the world!"

Why should we surrender to Satan whom Jesus
defeated on the cross? Why should we let this "lame
duck," whose time is short, rule over us? He lingers
on borrowed time; he is defeated! He will, of course,
make a ferocious last stand, but Jesus Christ will end
up victorious. In Revelation 15, we read of a
redeemed throng which in majestic splendor sings the
"song of Moses, the servant of God, and the song of the
Lamb" (v. 3). There "stood all those who had been
victorious over the Evil Creature" (v. 2). They had
triumphed over the devil.

No one can say with Hitler, "I will tear up
Christianity root and branch," or with John
Lennon, "We're [the Beatles] more popular than
Jesus," and remain impenitent without suffering sure
defeat. To oppose Jesus Christ is to incur ultimate defeat.
To accept him as Savior and follow him as Lord is to
know certain victory. Paul asked the Corinthians to
obey Christ "lest Satan should get an advantage of
us.... Now thanks be unto God, which always
causeth us to triumph in Christ" (2 Corinthians 2:11,
14, KJV).

The word of Christ defeats the devil. Mark wrote,

"Whenever those possessed by demons caught sight of him they would fall down before him shrieking, 'You are the Son of God' " (3:11). Matthew recounted, "That evening several demon-possessed people were brought to Jesus; and when he spoke a single word, all the demons fled" (8:16). It is important to note that it was when Jesus *spoke his Word* that the agents of Satan fled. This was always the case. In the Gospel of Luke we read that those who scrutinized closely the doings of Jesus were "amazed" and "asked, 'What is in this man's words that even demons obey him?' " (4:36).

The words of Jesus were always the Word of God, and the Word of God is always the word of Jesus, because "in these days [God] has spoken to us through his Son" (Hebrews 1:2). When Jesus resisted the devil's temptation by repeatedly quoting "It is written" (Matthew 4:4, 7, 10, KJV), he was simply quoting his own eternal Word. We read that "the devil leaveth him" (Matthew 4:11, KJV), for he had no other choice; he is subject to the Word of God.

Paul quickly learned about Satan's hatred for the Word of God. Right after his ordination to the ministry, he was sharing the gospel with a Roman governor who "desired to hear the Word of God," only to be militantly and belligerently withstood by a human "child of the devil" (Acts 13:7, 10, KJV).

One can hardly stress strongly enough how important it is that Christians read, study, pray over, meditate on, memorize, obey, and proclaim the Word of God. That's where we encounter our most furious and ferocious assaults from Satan, but it is the source of our greatest victories for the Lord. While Paul exhorted the Ephesian believers not to "give place to the devil" (4:27, KJV), he also told them to take up "the sword of the Spirit"—a defensive weapon—"which

165

is the word of God" (6:17, KJV). And he also wrote,
"Christ also loved the church, and gave himself for it;
that he might sanctify and cleanse it with the washing
of water by the word" (5:25, 26, KJV). So let us
wash our hearts clean with the Word of God as the
Scriptures command; let us eat the Word of God; let us
drink the Word of God. Let us give our lives to giving the
Word to our contemporaries, always aware of the fact
that when we do these things we will be opposed by
Satan.

There is a spiritual "energy crisis" today;
Christians seem to be unaware that they must be
energized by the Holy Spirit in order to overcome the
devil. Paul exhorted the Ephesians to wield the Word
(6:17). To the Thessalonians he wrote, "For our
gospel came not unto you in word only, but also in
power, and in the Holy Ghost" (1 Thessalonians 1:5,
KJV). Paul points out that as you face Satan, you
can't do so with an intellectual argument from the
Bible alone. You must at all times be sensitive to the
leadership of Christ by letting the Holy Spirit make the
Word of God real and plain to you. It is not a mere
academic exercise of memorizing a verse of Scripture,
followed by a clever intellectual application to a given
situation. There must be constant surrender to the
indwelling Christ. The Scriptures will always confirm
the revelation of the will of Christ to your heart when
the Holy Spirit is in charge of your life.

Jesus' whole ministry was a demonstration of
subduing Satan and his demons by being filled with the
Word and Spirit of God. Peter said, "Jesus of
Nazareth was anointed by God with the Holy Spirit
and with power, and he went around doing good and
healing all who were possessed by demons, for God was
with him" (Acts 10:38). There is no indication that Jesus
openly challenged the devil or his demons until he was

baptized by John in the Jordan River. According to Matthew, "After his baptism, as soon as Jesus came up out of the water, the heavens were opened to him and he saw the Spirit of God coming down in the form of a dove. And a voice from heaven said, 'This is my beloved Son, and I am wonderfully pleased with him.' Then Jesus was led out into the wilderness by the Holy Spirit, to be tempted there by Satan" (Matthew 3:16, 17; 4:1).

The sequence is significant. After being filled with the Holy Spirit, Jesus was subjected to the severest temptation Satan has ever leveled at anyone. He suffered indescribably, but there was not the slightest suggestion of acquiescence. Who, therefore, could be better qualified to stand by us when we are tossed into the floodwaters of temptation? For as the writer of Hebrews said, "For since he himself has now been through suffering and temptation, he knows what it is like when we suffer and are tempted, and he is wonderfully able to help us" (2:18).

But the point here is that he chose to provide a precedent, so that when we are called to face the devil, we too know we need to be filled with the Spirit. It is also significant that he cooperated with the Holy Spirit in all his miracles of exorcism, explaining candidly to his critics, "I am casting out demons by the Spirit of God" (Matthew 12:28). Later, in the days of the early church, there was sure to be an encounter with the devil and his demons wherever there was a fresh outpouring of the Holy Spirit. Shortly after the Holy Spirit said, "Dedicate Barnabas and Paul for a special job I have for them," they were directed to Cyprus where they encountered the sorcerer Bar-Jesus (Acts 13:2, 4).

One of the most familiar examples of a place where the Holy Spirit was poured out in momentous power was

167

Ephesus. It immediately became the target zone of the
devil. It was as though he had delegated a special
division of demons to disrupt the work of God.
When Paul arrived at Ephesus and got together with
the believers, he "laid his hands upon their heads [and]
the Holy Spirit came on them" (Acts 19:6). During Paul's
two-year ministry in that area, "God gave Paul the
power to do unusual miracles ... and any demons within
them came out" (19:11, 12). Were these demons
through making trouble? No. They waited for other
people to take them less seriously. When others tried
to imitate Paul, a demon "leaped on two of them and
beat them up, so that they fled ... naked and badly
injured" (19:16).

Don't play with the devil. Don't ever let your guard
down. If you are constantly sensitive to the guidance
of the Holy Spirit, there will be no room for the
devil to squeeze into your life. But he will try harder
than ever before to wield a little bit of influence. The
lesson here is that by being filled with the Holy Spirit,
you are victorious. Paul cautions, "Neither give place
to the devil" (Ephesians 4:27, KJV). He also urges,
"Be not drunk with wine, wherein is excess; but be
filled with the Spirit" (5:18, KJV).

Being filled with the Spirit is not an option, it is a
scriptural command. Victory over the devil depends on
it. Your effectiveness as a believer depends on it.
Without it you will fossilize. With it you will flourish!

Victory over the devil is something we never know
apart from prayer. And what a consolation it is to
know that our Lord himself is always praying for
us. Just before his trial Jesus addressed Peter:
"Simon, Simon, Satan has asked to have you, to sift
you like wheat, but I have pleaded in prayer for you that
your faith should not completely fail. So when you
have repented and turned to me again, strengthen and

build up the faith of your brothers" (Luke 22:31, 32). If
Peter the great apostle was dependent on the
prayers of Jesus, how much more are we. So let us
ever be faithful in prayer—for as we pray, our faith is
strengthened. The outcome is: "This is the victory that
overcometh the world, even our faith" (1 John 5:4,
KJV). Faith and prayer are inseparable. Wrote William
Cowper two centuries ago: "Prayer makes the
Christian's armor bright; and Satan trembles when
he sees the weakest saint upon his knees."

Sometimes, however, we falter in prayer and may
need to supplement our praying with fasting. While the
congregation of believers in Antioch prayed and
fasted, "the Holy Spirit said, 'Dedicate Barnabas and
Paul for a special job I have for them.' So after more
fasting and prayer, the men laid their hands on
them—and sent them on their way!" (Acts 13:2, 3).
Yes, fasting, prayer, and the power of the Holy Spirit
equipped Barnabas and Paul to go out victoriously and
evangelize the then known world.

The prayer and fasting combination as a preparation
for facing the devil was most evident in the life of our
Lord himself. We read that when he went "into the
wilderness to be tempted of the devil"—this was the
express purpose of his entry into the wilderness—that
he not only prayed but he "fasted forty days and forty
nights" (Matthew 4:1, 2, KJV). Luke noted that for
every hour of that time—not just afterwards when the
devil taunted our Lord with the three well-known
lures—"Satan tempted him for forty days" (Luke
4:1). Was it tough on Jesus, fasting? Indeed it was.
"He ate nothing all that time, and was very hungry."
But he was triumphant! And it is in his victory that we
stand triumphant over Satan.

Jesus indicated that both prayer and fasting are
necessary to defeat the devil and his cohorts. While

Jesus, Peter, James, and John were on the Mount of Transfiguration, a desperate father brought his demon-possessed son to the other disciples to have them exorcise the demon. Their efforts were a failure. But when Jesus himself came down, the man, who by now was crying, approached him. Jesus cast out the demon, and the helpless disciples asked him, " 'Why couldn't we cast that demon out?' 'Because of your faith,' Jesus told them.... 'This kind of demon won't leave unless you have prayed and gone without food' " (Matthew 17:19-21).

I have scores of missionary friends who are proclaiming Christ in Africa, Asia, South America, and Oceania. They relate to me fascinating—and somewhat frightening—accounts of demon possession against which every tactic seemed to fail. Then they took Jesus' exhortation and engaged in prayer and fasting. Only then could they demand in Jesus' name that the demon or demons come out.

We have not yet seen the open demonstration of demon possession in North America as some missionaries have seen it. But that is fast changing! I believe that we're going to have to add more fasting to our prayer in order to deal with the ever-worsening situation.

Victory over the devil through a strong prayer life can only be maintained by our constantly abiding in Christ. Christ living in us is a matter of spiritual reality; our living in Christ is a matter of carefully following him. Jesus instructed his disciples, "Abide in me, and I in you. As the branch cannot bear fruit of itself, except it abide in the vine; no more can ye, except ye abide in me" (John 15:4, KJV). In his letter to the Galatians, Paul urged Christians not to "follow your own wrong inclinations" such as "encouraging the activity of demons." No, they were instead to live in

the will of God, for "when the Holy Spirit controls
our lives he will produce this kind of fruit in us: love,
joy, peace, patience, kindness, goodness, faithfulness,
gentleness and self-control" (Galatians 5:19, 22, 23).

Some of us get very frustrated when we find
ourselves having to make important decisions. But in
this context Paul plainly taught that though "two
forces within us are constantly fighting each other
to win control over us, and our wishes are never free
from their pressures" (5:17), we are to follow the voice
of the Spirit. If we are willing to obey, then it is never a
problem for us to hear his voice.

"Abiding in the Lord" for victory is as old as history.
The author of Psalm 91 wrote of it: "We live within the
shadow of the Almighty, sheltered by the God who
is above all gods [demons].... You can safely meet a
lion or step on poisonous snakes, yes, even trample
them beneath your feet! For the Lord says, 'Because he
loves me, I will rescue him; I will make him great
because he trusts in my name' " (Psalm 91:1, 13, 14).
The Lord is interested in every detail of our lives, and
because he is, he sets before us an uncluttered
pathway. If we walk that pathway—at times it may
seem like a labyrinth—he will reward us with his
presence and blessing. And the word gets around. John
the Apostle wrote his congratulations to "you young
men ... because you have won your battle with Satan"
(1 John 2:13). They were living victorious Christian
lives because they had known and done the will of
Christ.

Living according to the will of Christ is no bed of
roses. Many times we feel the prick of thorns and
undergo, as Job did, real suffering. In fact, when Satan
turned his attention to Job, that ancient saint reached
rock bottom. But there he found the Bedrock of God's
providence. Plunged to the depths of his suffering

as he was, Job also knew the height of faith. He declared, "Though he slay me, yet will I trust in him" (Job 13:15, KJV).

Later the Apostle Paul wrote of another side of the coin. "I will say this: because these experiences I had were so tremendous, God was afraid I might be puffed up by them; so I was given a physical condition which has been a thorn in my flesh, a messenger from Satan to hurt and bother me, and prick my pride. Three times I begged God to make me well again. Each time he said, 'No. But I am with you; that is all you need. My power shows up best in weak people' " (2 Corinthians 12:7-9).

Peter also suffered at the hands of the devil. At the Last Supper (in the after-dinner talk that Jesus gave to his disciples), our Lord told Peter, "Satan hath desired to have you, that he may sift you as wheat" (Luke 22:31, KJV). But later the great apostle wrote, "that the trial of your faith, being much more precious than of gold that perisheth, though it be tried with fire, might be found unto praise and honor and glory at the appearing of Jesus Christ" (1 Peter 1:7, KJV).

And John, who sat closest to Christ during the Last Supper, wrote to the church at Smyrna, which was going through turbulent persecution, "I know how much you suffer for the Lord, and I know all about your poverty (but you have heavenly riches!). I know the slander of those opposing you, who say that they are Jews—the children of God—but they aren't, for they support the cause of Satan" (Revelation 2:9). John could afflict the comfortable when he saw them spiritually careless, but he could also comfort the afflicted when he knew they were being victimized by the devil.

But in all the persecution and suffering we may have to go through, we can be assured of peace and sanity of mind. As long as we reside in the will of Christ, our Lord promises us complete possession and stability of our mental faculties. When people were brought in faith to Jesus and "they were possessed by demons, or were insane, or paralyzed—he healed them all" (Matthew 4:24). In the case of the demoniac of Gadara, Luke the physician noted that the man's former acquaintances could hardly believe that they now "saw the man who had been demon-possessed sitting quietly at Jesus' feet, clothed and sane!" (8:35).

The devil is doing a great deal to derange people today. A *New York Times* article reasoned that there are more and more young people of the counterculture who reckon that human "life and existence are insane." Fifty-one percent of our hospital beds are occupied by people who have nothing organically wrong with them. The American Medical Association estimates that twenty-two million Americans suffer from mental illness. In Canada the admission rate of those entering psychiatric hospitals between 1960 and 1975 went up 300 percent. According to the Swedish Department of Social Affairs, 25 percent of the population of Sweden needs psychiatric treatment. Of course, all of these people are not demon-possessed. But I believe an increasingly large number of them will be as Satan emerges from behind his fronts. But even now the devil is indirectly responsible for much sickness—physical, mental, and spiritual.

We can expect Satan's forces to keep up a perpetual attack on our minds. But as believers in Christ we have the promise of the Word that "God hath not given us the spirit of fear; but of power, and of love, and of a sound mind" (2 Timothy 1:7, KJV).

What occupies your mind is very largely dependent on *who* occupies your mind! If Christ fills your thought life, Paul assured the Philippians, "you will experience God's peace, which is far more wonderful than the human mind can understand. His peace will keep your thoughts and your hearts quiet and at rest as you trust in Christ Jesus" (4:7). And what will be the content of your thought life when Jesus Christ is in residence? Paul went on to specify: "Fix your thoughts on what is true and good and right. Think about things that are pure and lovely, and dwell on the fine, good things in others. Think about all you can praise God for and be glad about. Keep putting into practice all you learned from me and saw me doing, and the God of peace will be with you" (4:8, 9).

Peace almost seems to be a lost commodity in today's world, but no Christian who is dwelling constantly in Christ need tolerate the turmoil Satan seeks to stir up. The devil is never happier than when he can rob a believer of peace.

Maintaining victory in all these areas involves constant vigilance. Jesus faced his great temptation from the devil and finally commanded, " 'Get out of here, Satan' ... Satan went away" (Matthew 4:10, 11). Some Greek scholars say that the phrase "Satan went away" could be paraphrased, "Satan sat back, merely stepped aside to await another chance to pounce."

Satan is constantly trying to catch us off-balance; he knows well that too many Christians too often let down their guard. The Apostle Peter warned, "Be careful—watch out for attacks from Satan, your great enemy. He prowls around like a hungry, roaring lion, looking for some victim to tear apart. Stand firm when he attacks. Trust the Lord; and remember that other Christians all around the world are going through these sufferings too" (1 Peter 5:8, 9). The devil, the prince of the power of the air that he is, always lurks on the horizon of your life to descend in awful spiritual storms and rip into your spiritual reserves. So never underestimate your enemy. Be vigilant!

But don't fear him. Resist him. "Resist the devil and he will flee from you," assured James (4:7). Paul, having just described the "strategies and tricks of Satan," admonished, "Resist the enemy whenever he attacks, and when it is all over, you will still be standing up" (Ephesians 6:11, 13). What a thrilling and wonderful promise!

Peter, who yielded to Satan when Jesus was nearing his death, later urged "Whom [the devil] resist steadfast in the faith" (1 Peter 5:9, KJV). An athletic team is never any stronger than the capacity of its defense to resist the opponent's offense. Spiritually, no matter how gifted you are or how many are your opportunities to serve Jesus Christ, you will never be any stronger against the devil than your determination and faith.

Many Christians, however, are so negative, so introspective, so intent on spiritual witch-hunting that they never positively present Jesus Christ as the only hope of the world. Using the analogy of the football game, they are so busy concentrating on defense that they fail to rally their offense so they can penetrate downfield for a touchdown.

Today begin an offensive attack for Christ. Invade your generation, your community, your immediate circle of friends, your family for Christ. Jesus commissioned his twelve disciples to go to "the people of Israel. Go and announce to them that the Kingdom of Heaven is near ... cast out demons. Give as freely as you have received!" (Matthew 10:7, 8). When Jesus had exorcised the "thousands" of demons out of the Gadarene, "the man who had been demon-possessed begged to go too [that is, he wanted just to travel with Jesus], but Jesus said no. 'Go back to your family,' he told him, 'and tell them what a

wonderful thing God has done for you.' So he went
all through the city telling everyone about Jesus' mighty
miracle'' (Luke 8:38, 39). It could be reasoned perhaps
that it was a dangerous thing indeed for Jesus to
unleash such a novice on his own townsfolk. But Jesus
doesn't make mistakes. As Ethel Waters puts it,
''Jesus don't sponsor no flops.'' The way for this
ex-demoniac to have spiritual victory was to obey
Jesus and go back home.

Constantly testifying for Jesus has a great deal to do
with a Christian's victory over the devil. Confess
Christ everywhere you go and your mind won't be idle,
''the devil's workshop.'' Wrote the Apostle John,
''Every spirit that confesseth not that Jesus Christ
is come in the flesh is ... of the world, and the world
heareth them. We are of God: he that knoweth God
heareth us; he that is not of God heareth not us. By this
know we the spirit of truth, and the spirit of error''
(1 John 4:3-6, KJV). Satan, of course, is behind any
spirit of error. He is *the* spirit of error.

Perhaps these planks in the platform of Christian
victory have never fit your experience. How, you
wonder, can anyone be victorious in a world of defeat,
disillusion, and despair? The answer is found in Christ,
but you feel the devil has you in his grip. But, wrote
John the Apostle, ''No one who has become part of
God's family makes a practice of sinning, for Christ,
God's Son, holds him securely and the devil cannot
get his hands on him'' (1 John 5:18). Moreover, the
apostle went on to state that you need not doubt
whether or not you are a child of God. ''We know that we
are children of God and that all the rest of the world
around us is under Satan's power and control'' (1 John
5:19).

The foundation for spiritual victory is this: Only
when we are members of God's family can we rest on

that Rock, Jesus Christ. And how does a person become a member of God's family? By a deliberate and decisive turning to Jesus Christ as one's Savior and Sovereign Lord. Paul reminded the Thessalonians "how you turned away from your idols [demon worship] to God so that now the living and true God only is your Master" (1 Thessalonians 1:9). Now the Thessalonians were victorious. Why? Because by the grace of God they had turned 180 degrees around: from demons to God; from Satan to the Savior; from their sins to salvation; from being dragged under to being lifted aloft. Counseled John Calvin, "If we desire to be united to Christ, we must of our own accord withdraw from the synagogue of Satan."

The Christian who levels with the devil and claims the Lordship of Jesus Christ is given these promises—and many more: "To everyone who is victorious, I will give fruit from the Tree of Life in the Paradise of God" (Revelation 2:7). "Everyone who is victorious shall eat of the hidden manna, the secret nourishment from heaven" (2:17). "As for the one who conquers, I will make him a pillar in the temple of my God; he will be secure, and will go out no more; and I will write my God's Name on him" (3:12). "To everyone who overcomes—who to the very end keeps on doing things that please me—I will give power over the nations" (2:26). "I will let everyone who conquers sit beside me on my throne, just as I took my place with my Father on his throne when I had conquered" (3:21). "Everyone who conquers will be clothed in white, and I will not erase his name from the Book of Life" (3:5). "Everyone who conquers will inherit all these blessings, and I will be his God and he will be my son" (21:7). No sacrifice can be too great considering that the reward for victory in Christ is described in those kinds of values. That's victory!

CHAPTER ELEVEN

When the Winning Begins

Our world is in trouble—and the trouble is basically spiritual. There is the raging, rampant drugs and narcotics epidemic, the VD pandemic, the blatant disregard for God's moral laws. There is corruption at all levels of society. Few absolutes seem to be left. A soaring wave of violence threatens to turn our homes into armed forts.

To a committed Christian, the most frightening aspect of all is the rising occult culture. The whole scene gives one a feeling of deep and growing concern that North America and Europe are heading straight toward judgment unless we, like Nineveh, repent and turn to God.

Despite our imperfections, inconsistencies, and injustices, the biblical basics of God's law and grace still provide the impetus for our moral and spiritual integrity—and an anchorage for our social, economic, and political conscience as a people under God. But like the leaning Tower of Pisa, our society is tipping further and further toward the point of collapsing.

There is a parallel in the book of Daniel. Daniel taught that a nation like ancient Persia can be all or partly controlled by the devil. He described "the mighty Evil Spirit [Satan]who overrules the kingdom of Persia" (Daniel 10:13), who held up the answer to his prayer for three weeks. During this time Daniel had been earnestly praying; suddenly he was struck to the ground in a deep faint. "But a hand touched me and lifted me, still trembling, to my hands and knees. And I heard his [an angel's] voice, 'O Daniel, greatly beloved of God,' he said, 'stand up and listen carefully to what I have to say to you, for God has sent me to you.' So I stood up, still trembling with fear.

"Then he said, 'Don't be frightened, Daniel, for your request has been heard in heaven and was answered the very first day you began to fast before the Lord and pray for understanding; that very day I was sent home to meet you. But for twenty-one days the mighty Evil Spirit who overrules the kingdom of Persia blocked my way. Then Michael, one of the top officers of the heavenly army, came to help me, so that I was able to break through these spirit rulers of Persia' " (Daniel 10:9-13).

This is what is very frightening indeed today, to a Bible believer. Is it possible that after all these years of divine blessing and protection North Americans are opening up to the forces of Satan, only to be cursed and defeated by him? We read in Daniel 12:1 that "Michael, the mighty angelic prince who stands guard over your nation, will stand up [and fight for you in heaven against satanic forces] (implied)." Evidently when people as a nation honor and love God, he shields and honors them by assigning a special angel of fairly high rank to look after their spiritual interests.

But it is alarming that most of the decisions in North American courts, schools, society at large, and in our entertainment have gone against Christ and his principles. It is a very serious thing for us as nations of the West to turn our backs on Jesus Christ. For when we abandon him and tip the balance against his rule in our nations, he withdraws that angelic oversight, and the evil spirit—that is, the devil, who ruled over ancient Persia for a while—will rule us. That is what distinguishes a nation with flagrant devil worship and witchcraft from nations like ours where historically satanic activity has been underground.

In Psalm 106, we read Jehovah's sobering warning to ancient Israel about their entanglements and involvement in the practices of devil-worshiping peoples. They "mingled in among the heathen and learned their evil ways, sacrificing to their idols [demon worship], and were led away from God. They even sacrificed their little children to the demons—the idols of Canaan—shedding innocent blood and polluting the land with murder. Their evil deeds defiled them, for their love of idols was adultery in the sight of God. That is why Jehovah's anger burned against his people, and he abhorred them. That is why he let the heathen nations crush them. They were ruled by those who hated them and oppressed by their enemies" (Psalm 106:35-42).

Is this a precedent for North America? The current spiritual drift on this continent bears an alarming resemblance to what happened to God's ancient people, Israel. The handwriting is unmistakably on the wall.

The result of apostasy is frightening to contemplate. Could it be that we are in danger of turning into a spiritual Babylon as identified, characterized, and described in

Revelation 18? Of course "Babylon" as here used is symbolic. But there are so many similarities that this amazing prophecy cannot be ignored. Nor is Revelation 18 the only chapter where the description and destruction of the "latter-day Babylon" is recorded.

Isaiah 47 is a parallel to Revelation 18—a prophecy which is both past and future. We read of a nation which was hooked on "demon hordes you've worshiped all these years." It was a "pleasure-mad kingdom" (vv. 12, 8). No modern society has ever gone so completely "pleasure-mad" as North America and Western Europe over the last few years, as we strive for less work and more leisure, not realizing how dehumanizing this is. We demand satisfaction for our appetites—we are on a sensuality binge. In our "pursuit of happiness," we extend ourselves to reach an increasingly elusive sense of fulfillment. And we're surfeiting ourselves so that we are losing all awareness of the temperance and discipline that society requires if it is to survive.

"You felt secure in all your wickedness" (v. 10). Probably one of the hardest tasks is that of warning a people of coming judgment, a judgment that many don't believe in because they don't want to believe. "Your 'wisdom' and 'knowledge' have caused you to turn away from me and claim that you yourself are Jehovah" (v. 10). One of the most monstrous sins is the deification of knowledge. What nation in history has ever had the laboratories, the libraries, the technological and scientific skills, and has experienced the leap forward, upward, and outward, that the United States has experienced during the last generation? The thermonuclear discoveries and inventions ... the computer ... the laser beam ... men on the moon ... and more breakthroughs to come!

Isaiah prophesied, "That is why disaster shall overtake you suddenly—so suddenly that you won't know where it comes from" (v. 11). It is ironic that our "knowledge" (or lack of it) is the reason why we cannot save ourselves from "disaster."

At a time like that, I can hear the nations say, "I alone am God! I'll never be a widow; I'll never lose my children" (v. 8). It seems to me that all we have to do is to look back over the last quarter of a century and see the nightmares which we call Korea and Vietnam and think of God's judgment. None of us—doves or hawks—liked it. How many lost children are there in those lands? How many widows are there whose husbands were taken from them by what were to many such meaningless and yet crazily inescapable wars?

Jesus described the signs of his second coming as "the beginning of sorrows" (Matthew 24:8, KJV).

John warns that "the sorrows of death and mourning and famine shall overtake her in a single day, and she shall be utterly consumed by fire" (Revelation 18:8). A nation wiped out in a single day? Impossible! It made no sense to people reading it before the 1940s. But with the advent of thermonuclear weapons, descriptions like this pose terrifying possibilities.

Where did ancient Israel go for help? "You have advisors by the ton—your astrologers and stargazers, who try to tell you what the future holds" (Isaiah 47:13). Theater groups, some of our athletic teams, a surprising number of our politicians, and even some of our clergymen are among the eight million North Americans who conduct their lives by the guidance they get from the "astrologers and stargazers." The Bible warns that while to the average person it is a game, or a "kick," it is not so to God!

These things appear on the surface to release supernatural power, but will they save any nation?

THE DEVIL

No! When Canada, America, Britain, Germany, or any other country ceases to be a "nation under God," you can write them off—unless they repent. "Behold, they shall be as stubble; the fire shall burn them; they shall not deliver themselves from the power of the flame" (v. 14, KJV). Before 1945, that warning of judgment upon a whole nation seemed like gross exaggeration. No one in his right mind today could for a moment dismiss it as unreality.

Sometimes when I am in a plane circling around for a landing at one of our airports, I see skylines of government and commercial buildings, loops of skyscrapers such as the world has never seen before. Then I think of the way idolatry, moral permissiveness, and crime are crowding out God. And to fill the enlarging vacuum, satanism, demon worship, and witchcraft are moving in.

I also think of Jesus' words when he was being ushered so triumphantly into Jerusalem—he knew they would crucify him within the week. He wept over a city he knew was doomed to judgment. "O Jerusalem, Jerusalem, the city that kills the prophets, and stones all those God sends to her! How often I have wanted to gather your children together as a hen gathers her chicks beneath her wings, but you wouldn't let me. And now your house is left to you, desolate" (Matthew 23:37). When I read a passage like that and look at the state of the world, I cannot help but have apprehensive thoughts about our future. How much longer can we expect God to stay his hand of judgment while our people refuse to repent? Especially is this true of those who know from the Bible that there is to be a major attempt by the devil to take over as we approach the end of the age.

As a people we must turn to God in repentance and be forgiven.

It's easy to wallow in pessimism, but the Bible promises that "greater is he that is in you, than he that is in the world" (1 John 4:4, KJV). The devil can never prevail where Jesus is enthroned and obeyed! Paul commended the Roman Christians, living in a society which resembles ours more and more, "Everyone knows that you stand loyal and true. This makes me very happy. I want you always to remain very clear about what is right, and to stay innocent of any wrong. The God of peace will soon crush Satan under your feet. The blessings from our Lord Jesus Christ be upon you" (Romans 16:19, 20). I believe that if we experience a spiritual revival throughout North America, Jesus Christ will soon crush Satan.

In the book of Numbers we find the story of Balaam, who lived on the banks of the Euphrates River near Babylon. I believe Balaam was a sorcerer. The Moabite king, Balak, was terrified of Israel. So he sent for Balaam, to have him curse Israel in the wilderness. Balak sent his top ambassadors who "begged Balaam to come and help" because "a vast horde of people has arrived from Egypt, and they cover the face of the earth and are headed toward me. Please come and curse them for me, so that I can drive them out of my land; for I know what fantastic blessings fall on those whom you bless, and I also know that those whom you curse are doomed" (22:6).

Balaam tried to curse Israel, but he found that "Jehovah their God is with them. He is their king! God has brought them out of Egypt ... no curse can be placed on Jacob, and no magic shall be done against him" (23:21-23). Balaam found out that when God is blessing a people, the devil has no real power. That's the way it could be here in North America or in any country where the people give Christ first place.

Christ is committed to his Word, which promises he

will protect his church from the devil. He declared to Peter one day while he was on earth, "I will build my church; and all the powers of hell [the Devil and his hordes of demons] shall not prevail against it." He didn't say he would build secular-religious organizations; he said, "I will build my church... And I will give you the keys of the Kingdom of Heaven; whatever doors you lock on earth shall be locked in heaven; and whatever doors you open on earth shall be open in heaven!" (Matthew 16:18, 19).

What is the Christian's role in this? Christ is the "Key," so we must give ourselves to him by repentance and faith. We need to pray that the devil will be bound. Jesus taught that "Satan must be bound before his demons are cast out, just as a strong man must be tied up before his house can be ransacked and his property robbed" (Mark 3:27). We should pray individually for victory. But there is special promise of victory when two or more of us pray together. Jesus taught his disciples, "And I tell you this— whatever you bind on earth is bound in heaven, and whatever you free on earth will be freed in heaven. I also tell you this—if two of you agree down here on earth concerning anything you ask for, my Father in heaven will do it for you. For where two or three gather together because they are mine, I will be right there among them" (Matthew 18:18-20).

Today the greatest service any Christian can do for God, country, and home is to call people together for prayer. Pray in Jesus' name that the strongholds of Satan will be invaded, subdued, and bound. Pray that as a people we will turn back to the faith of our fathers and forward to new spiritual frontiers. Pray for an awakening which will spread across this continent and to the world, a revival that will hold the Lord's hand of judgment for a time.

The church's second priority in the offensive against the devil is to realize that as we abide in Christ and obey him, we can recognize Satan for what he is, a deceiver and a masterful fraud. "I know the slander of those opposing you," declared the Lord to those of the church in Smyrna. They may say "that they are Jews—the children of God—but they aren't, for they support the cause of Satan" (Revelation 2:9). Paul wrote to the Corinthians that God the Holy Spirit gives the "power to know whether evil spirits are speaking through those who claim to be giving God's messages—or whether it is really the Spirit of God who is speaking" (1 Corinthians 12:10).

The devil often oversteps himself. He did in apostolic times. He incited Saul of Tarsus to such hostility against Christ that he "was like a wild man, going everywhere to devastate the believers, even entering private homes and dragging out men and women alike and jailing them" (Acts 8:3). But later this devil-driven wild man was translated "out of the darkness and gloom of Satan's kingdom and brought ... into the kingdom of his dear Son" (Colossians 1:13).

This Apostle Paul underscored for us a third priority: Put Christ and his love first and Satan cannot ever separate you from Christ. "For I am convinced that nothing can ever separate us from his love. Death can't, and life can't. The angels won't, and all the powers of hell itself cannot keep God's love away" (Romans 8:38). And when the devil attempts to trespass, the Lord himself has promised that he "will be a swift witness against the sorcerers" (Malachi 3:5, KJV). Young people need to begin now to go all out for Christ. Alexander Pope once said, "When men grow virtuous in their old age, they only make a sacrifice to God of the devil's leavings." Whatever your age, start now for Christ.

THE DEVIL

Paul gives us yet another priority. In our witness for Christ, we are boldly to make the message clear and plain. But we are not to try to do the Holy Spirit's work. Bringing spiritual conviction to a man's heart is the prerogative of the Holy Spirit. The Christian must be careful to speak to people with a "holy" boldness, for if he speaks "meekly and courteously to them they are more likely, with God's help, to turn away from their wrong ideas and believe what is true. Then they will come to their senses and escape from Satan's trap of slavery to sin which he uses to catch them whenever he likes, and then they can begin doing the will of God. You may as well know this too, Timothy, that in the last days it is going to be very difficult to be a Christian," for among other things, "evil men and false teachers will become worse and worse, deceiving many, they themselves having been deceived by Satan" (2 Timothy 2:25, 26; 3:1, 13). Here the balance in our witness is expressed. Our witness is to be bold, but considerate; gracious, and with love.

In the future it is going to be so difficult for those who take their stand for Christ that a great number are going to have to put their lives on the line. They will die, but their death will be an overcoming death. In the book of Revelation, John reveals that there is coming a day when "the devil, or Satan, the one deceiving the whole world" will be so blatantly murderous of Christians that he'll have them slaughtered right, left, and center. But no matter—"they defeated him by the blood of the Lamb, and by their testimony; for they did not love their lives but laid them down for him. Rejoice, O heavens! You citizens of heaven, rejoice!" (Revelation 12:9, 11, 12).

This rejoicing in heaven leads us to another priority in our conflict with the devil. Jesus said that always "there is joy in the presence of the angels of God

188

when one sinner repents" (Luke 15:10)—he is snatched from the power of Satan. Jesus assures ultimate victory, but it is never to be a matter of pride. Jesus' disciples tended to make that mistake. We read that "when the seventy disciples returned, they joyfully reported to him, 'Even the demons obey us when we use your name' " (Luke 10:17). But Jesus gave them a gentle rebuke—"Rejoice not that the spirits are subject unto you; but rather rejoice, because your names are written in heaven" (10:20, KJV).

Is your name written in heaven? This is the most important question any person in the world ever faces! Paul challenged the Corinthian church, "Check up on yourselves. Are you really Christians? Do you pass the test? Do you feel Christ's presence and power more and more within you? Or are you just pretending to be Christians when actually you aren't at all?" (2 Corinthians 13:5). He had warned them earlier that ordinances and ritual can't save, nor can baptism save. He also cautioned them that when they sat down to share a communion service, they must keep solemnly in mind that "you cannot drink from the Lord's Table and at Satan's table, too. You cannot eat bread both at the Lord's Table and at Satan's table" (1 Corinthians 10:21).

Centuries earlier, Joshua had thrown out the challenge, "Choose you this day whom ye will serve" (Joshua 24:15, KJV). He did not say "*what* ye will serve," but "*whom* ye will serve." As for Joshua, he would not serve the devil. He vowed, "As for me and my house, we will serve the Lord." Elijah the prophet made the same point. "How long are you going to waver between two opinions?" he asked Israel. "If the Lord is God, *follow* him! But if Baal is God, then follow *him!*" (1 Kings 18:21). Today people in their moments of truth realize they have a definite choice to

189

make; the lines are sharply drawn. Alan Watts, in a
Time article on the devil, made it plain that sorcery
and demonism of all forms offer an alternative to
the Christian way.

God has never permitted spiritual fence-walking.
There is no "no-man's-land" or middle ground. In
Ezekiel we read, "O Israel, the Lord God says: If you
insist on worshiping your idols, go right ahead, but then
don't bring your gifts to me as well!" (20:39). There is
no way a man can have Christ and the devil at the
same time, any more than he can go to heaven and to
hell at the same time.

The issue of eternal life rests squarely on what a man
does with Jesus Christ. It is how he votes when he
enters with his soul into the polling booth of his will.
Always and ever, the matter of salvation is
decided—not on which religious denomination we
choose, not on which set of religious doctrines we
adopt or our particular religious creed—but on Pilate's
age-old dilemma, "What shall I do then with Jesus which
is called Christ?" (Matthew 27:22, KJV). It boils down
to a deliberate choice between Jesus and Satan. It is as
simple and inescapable as that!

Jesus made this clear. He said, "He that is not with me
is against me" (Matthew 12:30, KJV). On another
occasion, Jesus declared, "Neither you nor anyone else
can serve two masters. You will hate one and show
loyalty to the other, or else the other way around—
you will be enthusiastic about one and despise
the other. You cannot serve God and money"
(Luke 16:13). The two mutually exclude each other,
as do Christ and Satan.

I ask you now, wherever you are, to receive Jesus
Christ into your life, if you have not already done so.
There are two forces at work in our world—Christ
and the devil. And you are asked to choose. Whether

you know it or like it, if you are not Christ's you are in a
spiritual voting booth. You have to cast a vote. The devil
is campaigning to remain incumbent. The crusade is
for your soul. Christ paid the redemption cost to
purchase your peace and pardon. But you, and you
alone, must cast your vote. Who are you going to
follow, Christ or the devil?

As *The New York Times* said, Dr. George Faust is
only the most notorious and most representative of the
millions in history who have "traded their immortal
souls to Satan for wealth, power, knowledge, and
pleasure." In contrast, Lady Ann Erskine was, two
centuries ago, the most influential female Christian
in Scotland. She became a great force for Christ
when she was a beautiful young woman. It all began one
day when she was out riding in her regal bedecked coach.
She saw a large crowd assembled. She tapped her
coachman on the shoulder and asked, "Who is that man
addressing that huge gathering, there in the open air?"
She was told that it was Rowland Hill, the great
Welsh preacher.

"Drive over and let me hear what this curious fellow
has to say!" she instructed. As she pulled up, Rowland
Hill immediately recognized her. He stopped for a
moment and turned boldly toward her. Fearlessly he
declared, "I have something for sale! It is Lady Ann
Erskine's soul! Who will bid? Yes, Satan! What is
your offer? 'I will give riches, honor, and pleasure!'
shouts the devil.

"Jesus Christ speaks up: 'I will give eternal life!' "

Lady Ann Erskine was angry. But superseding her
indignation was the unmistakable call of Christ to her
soul. She descended the gilded steps of her coach and
knelt beside a gleaming wheel on the turf. She cried
out, "I will have Jesus!" And Scotland has never
been quite the same since.

Resolve in your heart now, as Lady Ann Erskine did, "I will have Jesus! I want him to forgive my sins. I want him to write my name in the Book of Life." You may be a member of the church. You may be Catholic, Protestant, Orthodox, Jewish, some other religion, or a member of no religion. Jesus Christ will come into your heart right now if you will invite him.

Christmas Evans was another of the great Welsh preachers two centuries ago. One night he declared dramatically to a vast audience that the devil had a conference in hell. He told his demon army that there was a great Christian revival on the earth and that the people were turning to Christ in such numbers that something had to be done to stop it. Were there any ideas? One demon spoke up and said, "Let's attack the Bible, the book that carries the message of salvation!" A second suggested, "Let's attack the ministers who are preaching salvation through faith in Christ!" Another said, "Let's attack the fact that people can be saved at all through faith in Christ!" Each of these got a demonic cheer and a nod from the devil. Finally the deputy to the devil spoke up: "We've tried all these things, but here's the best one. Let's concede all these points and simply whisper into the ears of all who are about to be converted, 'Yes, be converted, but not now!' " The devil brought down his gavel. "That's it!" he affirmed.

The devil is saying to you who have not decided for Christ, "Yes, but not now! Yes, but not now! Yes, but not now!"

But you must not listen to him. Pray this prayer now: "God be merciful to me, a sinner, and save me now for Christ's sake. Deliver me from the power of the devil. Enable me by your grace to live the Christian life until you call me home or come for me. I thank you, Lord Jesus Christ."